Systemic Bias

Systemic Bias: Algorithms and Society looks at issues of computational bias in the contexts of cultural works, metaphors of magic and mathematics in tech culture, and workplace psychometrics.

The output of computational models is directly tied not only to their inputs but to the relationships and assumptions embedded in their model design, many of which are of a social and cultural, rather than physical and mathematical, nature. How do human biases make their way into these data models, and what new strategies have been proposed to overcome bias in computed products?

Scholars and students from many backgrounds as well as policy makers, journalists, and the general reading public will find a multidisciplinary approach to inquiry into algorithmic bias encompassing research from Communication, Art, and New Media.

Michael Filimowicz is Senior Lecturer in the School of Interactive Arts and Technology (SIAT) at Simon Fraser University. He has a background in computer-mediated communications, audiovisual production, new media art, and creative writing. His research develops new multimodal display technologies and forms, exploring novel form factors across different application contexts including gaming, immersive exhibitions, and simulations.

Algorithms and Society

Series Editor:
Dr Michael Filimowicz *is Senior Lecturer in the School of Interactive Arts and Technology (SIAT) at Simon Fraser University.*

As algorithms and data flows increasingly penetrate every aspect of our lives, it is imperative to develop sufficient theoretical lenses and design approaches to humanize our informatic devices and environments. At stake are the human dimensions of society which stand to lose ground to calculative efficiencies and performance, whether at the service of government, capital, criminal networks, or even a general mob concatenated in social media.

Algorithms and Society is a new series which takes a broad view of the information age. Each volume focuses on an important thematic area, from new fields such as software studies and critical code studies to more established areas of inquiry such as philosophy of technology and science and technology studies. This series aims to stay abreast of new areas of controversy and social issues as they emerge with the development of new technologies.

If you wish to submit a book proposal for the series, please contact Dr Michael Filimowicz michael_f@sfu.ca or Emily Briggs emily.briggs@tandf.co.uk

Digital Totalitarianism
Algorithms and Society
Edited by Michael Filimowicz

Privacy
Algorithms and Society
Edited by Michael Filimowicz

Systemic Bias
Algorithms and Society
Edited by Michael Filimowicz

Democratic Frontiers
Algorithms and Society
Edited by Michael Filimowicz

Deep Fakes
Algorithms and Society
Edited by Michael Filimowicz

For more information on the series, visit: https://www.routledge.com/Algorithms-and-Society/book-series/ALGRAS

Systemic Bias
Algorithms and Society

**Edited by
Michael Filimowicz**

Routledge
Taylor & Francis Group

LONDON AND NEW YORK

First published 2022
by Routledge
4 Park Square, Milton Park, Abingdon, Oxon OX14 4RN

and by Routledge
605 Third Avenue, New York, NY 10158

Routledge is an imprint of the Taylor & Francis Group, an informa business

British Library Cataloguing-in-Publication Data
A catalogue record for this book is available from the British Library

Library of Congress Cataloging-in-Publication Data
A catalog record has been requested for this book

ISBN: 978-1-032-00255-2 (hbk)
ISBN: 978-1-032-00257-6 (pbk)
ISBN: 978-1-003-17337-3 (ebk)

DOI: 10.4324/9781003173373

Typeset in Times New Roman
by codeMantra

Contents

Figures

Contributors

Eleanor Dare lectures at the Faculty of Education, Cambridge University. Eleanor is an academic and critical technologist with a PhD and an MSc in Arts and Computational Technologies from the Department of Computing, Goldsmiths. Eleanor was formerly Reader in Digital Media and Head of Programme for MA Digital Direction at the Royal College of Art.

Christophe Magis is Associate Professor of Political Economy of Communications and Director of the Master Program on Music Business Management at the Université Paris 8 (France). His research interests include the critical political economy of cultural and communication industries and the epistemology of critical theories in communication. He is currently working on the topic "(Pre-)Histories of the culture industry and transformations of ideology".

Jakob Svensson is Professor in Media and Communication Studies at Malmö University, Sweden. He is currently finishing a research project funded by the Swedish research council on people and cultures behind algorithms and automated systems. Other research interests revolve around mobile phones and empowerment in the Global South, as well as digital media and political communication.

Dr. Dylan Yamada-Rice is a Senior Lecturer in Immersive Storytelling in the School of Digital Arts at Manchester Metropolitan University. She is also an artist and researcher specializing in play and stories for children. She is currently working as a Co-Investigator on an EPSRC-funded project "Countermeasures" focused on finding creative ways to increase children's awareness of, and agency over, the sensors embedded in everyday digital devices.

Series Preface
Algorithms and Society

Michael Filimowicz

This series is less about what algorithms are and more about how they act in the world through "eventful" (Bucher, 2018, p. 48) forms of "automated decision making" (Noble, 2018, loc. 141) in which computational models are "based on choices made by fallible human beings" (O'Neil, 2016, loc. 126).

> Decisions that used to be based on human reflection are now made automatically. Software encodes thousands of rules and instructions computed in a fraction of a second.
>
> (Pasquale, 2015, loc. 189)

> If, in the industrial era, the promise of automation was to displace manual labor, in the information age it is to pre-empt agency, spontaneity, and risk: to map out possible futures before they happen so objectionable ones can be foreclosed and desirable ones selected.
>
> (Andrejevic, 2020, p. 8)

> [M]achine learning algorithms that anticipate our future propensities are seriously threatening the chances that we have to make possible alternative political futures.
>
> (Amoore, 2020, p. xi)

Algorithms, definable pragmatically as "a method for solving a problem" (Finn, 2017, loc. 408), "leap from one field to the next" (O'Neil, 2016, loc. 525). They are "*hyperobjects*: things with such broad temporal and spatial reach that they exceed the phenomenological horizon of human subjects" (Hong, 2020, p. 30). While in the main, the technological systems taken up as volume topics are design solutions to problems for which there are commercial markets, organized communities, or claims of state interest, their power and ubiquity generate new problems for inquiry. The series will do its part to track this domain fluidity across its volumes and contest, through critique and investigation, their "logic of secrecy" (Pasquale, 2015, loc. 68), and "obfuscation" (loc. 144).

These new *social* (rather than strictly computational) problems that are generated can, in turn, be taken up by many critical, policy, and speculative discourses. At their most productive, such debates can potentially alter the ethical, legal, and even imaginative parameters of the environments in which the algorithms of our information architectures and infrastructures operate, as algorithmic implementations often reflect a "desire for epistemic purity, of knowledge stripped of uncertainty and human guesswork" (Hong, 2020, p. 20). The series aims to foster a general intervention in the conversation around these often "black boxed" technologies and track their pervasive effects in society.

> Contemporary algorithms are not so much transgressing settled societal norms as establishing new patterns of good and bad, new thresholds of normality and abnormality, against which actions are calibrated.
>
> (Amoore, 2020, p. 5)

Less "hot button" algorithmic topics are also of interest to the series, such as their use in the civil sphere by citizen scientists, activists, and hobbyists, where there is usually not as much discursive attention. Beyond private, state, and civil interests, the increasingly sophisticated technology-based activities of criminals, whether amateur or highly organized, deserve broader attention as now everyone must defend their digital identities. The information systems of companies and states conduct a general form of "ambient surveillance" (Pasquale, 2015, loc. 310), and anyone can be a target of a hacking operation.

Algorithms and Society thus aims to be an interdisciplinary series which is open to researchers from a broad range of academic backgrounds. While each volume has its defined scope, chapter contributions may come from many areas such as sociology, communications, critical legal studies, criminology, digital humanities, economics, computer science, geography, computational media and design, philosophy of technology, and anthropology, along with others. Algorithms are "shaping the conditions of everyday life" (Bucher, 2018, p. 158) and operate "at the intersection of computational space, cultural systems, and human cognition" (Finn, 2017, loc. 160), so the multidisciplinary terrain is vast indeed.

Since the series is based on the shorter Routledge Focus format, it can be nimble and responsive to emerging areas of debate in fast-changing technological domains and their sociocultural impacts.

References

Amoore, L. (2020). *Cloud Ethics: Algorithms and the Attributes of Ourselves and Others*. Duke University Press.

Andrejevic, M. (2020). *Automated Media*. Taylor and Francis.

Bucher, T. (2018). *If...Then: Algorithmic Power and Politics*. Oxford University Press.

Finn, E. (2017). *What Algorithms Want: Imagination in the Age of Computing*. MIT Press. Kindle version.

Hong, S. H. (2020). *Technologies of Speculation: The Limits of Knowledge in a Data-Driven Society*. New York University Press.

Noble, S. U. (2018). *Algorithms of Oppression*. New York University Press. Kindle version.

O'Neil, C. (2016). *Weapons of Math Destruction*. Broadway Books. Kindle version.

Pasquale, F. (2015). *The Black Box Society*. Harvard University Press. Kindle version.

Volume introduction

Michael Filimowicz

The issue of systemic bias is perhaps the most well-known research area in studies on the impacts of algorithm design and implementation on society. The chapters in this volume chart new lines of inquiry into bias, expanding this theme into cultural works, tech culture, and workplace psychometrics.

Chapter 1 – "From 'Diversity' to 'Discoverability': Platform Economy, Algorithms, and the Transformations of Cultural Policies" by Christophe Magis – examines semantic shifts from the guiding concept of cultural diversity to discoverability in the context of new streaming platforms and their recommendation algorithms. These shifts in meaning have important consequences for digital culture as they impact on policy, economic, and political levels.

Chapter 2 – "Modern Mathemagics: Values and Biases in Tech Culture" by Jakob Svensson – examines tech culture mythologies termed *mathemagics*: a modern enchantment with software's capacity to manipulate, control, and spur progress in the world. Drawing on the 16th-century philosopher-theologian Bruno, these magic metaphors promise to make possible the impossible and risk the emergence of evil in the real world.

Chapter 3 – "Reading the Cards: Critical Chatbots, Tarot and Drawing as an Epistemological Repositioning to Defend Against the Neoliberal Structures of Art Education" by Eleanor Dare and Dylan Yamada-Rice – brings to light the increasing and problematic use of automated psychometrics in higher education, including personality and behavioral metrics, facial recognition, sound analysis, and eye tracking. These tools are increasingly being favored in the NeoLiberal University, and the authors urge resistance through specific creative methodologies.

Acknowledgment

The chapter summaries here have in places drawn from the authors' chapter abstracts, the full versions of which can be found in Routledge's online reference for the volume.

1 From "Diversity" to "Discoverability"

Platform Economy, Algorithms and the Transformations of Cultural Policies

Christophe Magis

In a recent article in *The Economist*, one reads:

> An irony of European integration is that it is often American com-
> panies that facilitate it. Google Translate makes European news-
> papers comprehensible, even if a little clunky, for the continent's
> non-polyglots. American social-media companies make it easier
> for Europeans to talk politics across borders. [...] Now Netflix
> and friends pump the same content into homes across a continent,
> making culture a cross-border endeavour, too.[1]

The columnist, who further portrays European executives and politicians as conservative fighters for cultural sovereignty who need to op-
pose American cultural hegemony, does not find it relevant to mention
how the American giants at the core of the platform economy such as
Google, Facebook or Amazon have short-changed the EU countries
enormous sums in tax avoidance for this so-called aid. Furthermore,
while cultural platforms such as Netflix could be said to have encour-
aged cultural change more than politicians themselves, their algorithmic systems of recommendation are leading to major transformations
in cultural policy. This chapter focuses on such a transformation in
the French-speaking world. Whereas France and Québec have been
active defenders of "diversity" in negotiations between the supranational institutions and in their own domestic policies, they have recently collaborated in the shift towards "discoverability". Based on
an analysis of the scholarly literature and official reports from national and supranational institutions, this chapter retraces the history
of semantic shifts in cultural policy from "cultural exceptionalism"
and "diversity" to "discoverability", and demonstrates that this movement, primarily dictated by a pragmatic reaction to the importance

DOI: 10.4324/9781003173373-1

that algorithms have acquired in cultural life, has huge consequences on the sociopolitical and socioeconomic levels. This shift can also be analyzed in correlation with the general decline in the critical theory underlying cultural policies.

"Cultural diversity": academic and institutional history of a polysemic notion

The theme of *cultural diversity* has been given place of honor in political discourse on culture over the last 20 years, especially since it was proposed by supranational institutions such as UN Educational, Scientific and Cultural Organization (UNESCO) or the EU.[2] It has also been a central category in academic discourse, in many works on culture, media and communications. Indeed, as Tristan Mattelart (2011, 29) writes, "the notion of 'cultural diversity' appears to be self-evident. How could one be against the pluralism it implies"? But the author also points out how polysemic the term is, problematic in that it is exploited by divergent political agendas and opposing theoretical projects. This first section studies this polysemy through the analysis of its adoption in both academic and institutional discourse.

The threat posed by globalization for the cultural autonomy of many Third World countries—in particular newly independent states—has been the subject of several critical studies since the late 1960s, especially in the political economy of communication, alongside issues concerning the growing concentration of media ownership (see Magis 2020 for an overview). Drawing on several critical—usually Marxian—concepts, these studies have advocated the development of national or regional media policies to help such countries develop their own offer in a situation of *unequal exchange* (Emmanuel 1972) and avoid *cultural homogenization* (Schiller 1970, 1976; A. Mattelart 1976). More generally, they have also argued for stronger cultural industries and media regulation. It was only when the UN finally addressed the theme of the globalization of culture (beginning in the mid-1970s) that the notion of "cultural diversity" was defined.

Such relative institutionalization has led to further analysis and a broadening of theoretical frameworks. On the one hand, the notion of "cultural diversity" has legitimized other critical works on cultural dependency (notably concerning television and cinema). For example, in a 1974 report, Kaarle Nordenstreng and Tapio Väris observe how much "national" television programs consist mainly of imports from the US, especially for entertainment (Nordenstreng and Väris 1974; see also

A. Mattelart, Delcourt, and M. Mattelart 1984). Subsequently, some authors have endorsed policies in favor of safeguarding "national sovereignty" in communication (Nordenstreng and Schiller 1979) or "cultural autonomy" (Hamelink 1983). On the other hand, "diversity" has also become the category in which these works have been contested, in particular by postmodernist theorists. While culture has tended to become a profitable sector of investment for the capital of investors from developed countries, postmodernist studies and reports have assimilated voluntarist and autonomist cultural policies to a protectionist nationalism leading to a more impoverished cultural offer (e.g., Pool 1977). Furthermore, a change of perspective occurred in the 1980s: the idea that cultural diversity was produced through the *consumption* of (global) cultural commodities. As T. Mattelart (2011, 26) observes, this change of perspective is largely associated with the development of scholarly work on television. Such discourses have aimed at countering the threat that a transnational circulation of cultural products poses to national and cultural identities by examining how the reception of the same cultural program can be regionally "diverse":

> The world capitalist system was represented in the works of critical political economy in the 1970s and in the early 1980s as producing cultural standardization. Since the late 1980s, it is increasingly described as generating cultural diversity, even if placed under the sign of commodification.
>
> (T. Mattelart 2008, 48)

Thus redefined, "diversity" has become an important institutional category. It has been used in the construction of media indexes, such as the American Federal Communications Commission's Diversity Index (Downing 2011), and has assumed an important place in international negotiations concerning cultural and media industries from the 1990s onwards. It has gradually replaced the rhetoric of "cultural exceptionalism"—which dominated General Agreement on Tariffs and Trade (GATT; later World Trade Organization [WTO])[3] trade talks until the late 1980s—with a positive slogan articulating regional media lobbying with a narrative on indigenous cultural richness, under the auspices of UNESCO. Indeed, after the First World War, Hollywood was feared by many European governments for its economic and cultural impact, resulting in various measures to protect and stimulate domestic production. France, in particular, was a notable advocate of these measures, pursued under the policy of "exception culturelle" by the minister of culture André Malraux. The first GATT treaty in 1947 validated such measures for films (GATT Article IV), followed by regional agreements: the EU, where France has been very proactive, especially when Jacques Delors presided the European Commission and "acted as a strong policy entrepreneur, reflecting as well as shaping the views of the member states" (Burri 2015, 199) or, under a Canadian initiative, the Canada-United States Free Trade Agreement (1988) and the North American Free Trade Agreement (1994). France and Canada, both economically significant cultural producers and defenders of the French language through the *Organisation internationale de la Francophonie* (OIF—"International Francophonie Organization"), have then actively worked towards advancing the idea of *cultural exceptionalism* at the Organisation for Economic Co-Operation and Development (OECD) in 1998 and at the Seattle WTO summit (1999). But, as the former ambassador—and major participant in French international lobbying—Jean Musitelli (2006, 2) explains, "it became apparent that Cultural Exception[alism] was not only insufficient protection, but also a standard that did not inspire much call to action". Furthermore:

> Cultural Exception[alism] was perceived, by developing countries, as a barrier erected by Europeans against the invasion of their audio-visual and film markets by the US leisure industry. They did not feel overly concerned by this war of images among the well-to-do.

Therefore France, soon followed by Canada, suggested replacing it with the notion of "cultural diversity" in debates: "opening up the narrow field of vision of exception[alism] onto a broadened horizon", the notion of diversity "rehabilitated the anthropological and sociological components of culture which had been ignored in commercial negotiations" (Ibid.). Like its academic counterpart, the notion was thus emptied of any normative significance (A. Mattelart 2005) and therefore of true operational scope and henceforth promoted through UNESCO declarations—especially the "Universal Declaration on Cultural Diversity" (2001) or the "Convention on the Protection and Promotion of the Diversity of Cultural Expressions" (2005). In phase with the demands of some regional groups for better representation in global cultural programs and thus promoted as a corollary of *biological* diversity, the term abandoned its initial impulse to attack media concentration through the regulation of media's economic structures (McChesney 2008). On the contrary, following the American wave of deregulation—of which the Telecommunications Act (1996) is paradigmatic—many EU discussions of the late 1990s and the 2000s argued that building European media giants capable of counterbalancing American counterparts was the best way of protecting and promoting diversity, mistaking an abundance of programs with diversity of content (Bouquillion 2008). Thus, "cultural diversity" was also welcomed by global producers: in the early 2000s, Vivendi Universal's president Jean-Marie Messier stated: "We are now in a period of cultural diversity. What does that mean? It means we must be both global and national".[4] A distinctive socioeconomic feature of the cultural industries is "overproduction" as an organizational way of coping with structural demand uncertainty (Hirsch 1972; Doyle 2002); labeling this oversupply as "diversity" has thus been an easy way of promoting the major cultural producers.

Measuring diversity: democracy through the lens of cultural capitalism

As we have seen, the history of "cultural diversity" is that of an impoverishment of its critical impulses, with the rise of neoliberalism in cultural policies and of postmodernism in academic debate. Its institutionalization through supranational organizations has been realized at the expense of reforming media structures. Nevertheless, such institutionalization has also led to research interest across many disciplines. Thus, even negatively, the notion has maintained an ideal of democracy, although in general not explicitly.

In France, in the last 20 years "cultural diversity" has been the subject of many theoretical and methodological discussions in the field of cultural economics (Benhamou 2006; Greffe 2006); at the same time, it has been widely used in official reports on cultural activity. Since the turn of the 21st century, the Département des études de la prospective et des statistiques (DEPS—"Department for Surveys, Strategic Forecasts and Statistics") of the French Ministry of Culture and Communication regularly publishes sectorial studies on the evolution of diversity in cultural industries. The British Department for Culture, Media and Sports (DCMS—renamed Department for Digital, Culture, Media and Sports in 2017) has also funded comparable studies. In 2004, a special issue of the *Journal of Media Economics* was devoted to the theoretical analysis of the category of "cultural diversity".

These theoretical developments in cultural economics have rapidly faltered over the problem of *measuring* cultural diversity. Contrary to corporate discourse, diversity cannot obviously be identified with the number of different titles produced, since it concerns a sector where an abundance of supply is a structural characteristic. Drawing on indicators from biology (in particular, Rao 1982), cultural economists have finally agreed on three criteria: *variety* (quantity of titles produced), *balance* (homogeneity in the sales of titles) and *disparity* (the degree of difference between different titles), following a model first proposed by Andrew Stirling (1998). All else being equal, diversity increases with the increment of the three variables. But if "[t]he quantitative assessment of variety and balance is straightforward: variety is a simple positive integer, and balance is something close to variance", the same cannot be said for the third indicator: "disparity turns out to be much more difficult to assess" (Moreau and Peltier 2004, 126). If the methodological debate continues amongst cultural economists—where some simply avoid the question of disparity—researchers have reached general agreement on a set of local variables for measuring each indicator. For instance, a study on "cultural diversity in the French recording industry" commissioned by the DEPS settles on 11 variables for assessing disparity, such as "renewal rate in the top titles", "similarity ratio between tops and circuits" or the "number of active publishers" (Bourreau, Moreau, and Senellart 2011). With local differences depending on the cultural sectors under analysis, this model was influential in the different reports commissioned by institutions such as UNESCO or national governments. A more recent trend, required by the overabundance of supply in digital ecosystems, further distinguishes between *produced* (or *supplied*) diversity and *consumed* diversity (Napoli 2011).

The parameters of diversity have been and continue to be a central point of debate. Indeed, its three main indicators and their subsequent variables pose several crucial methodological problems. The above-mentioned variables used in official reports for determining disparity in the recording industry are somewhat tautological: instead of an actual evaluation of difference, they measure concentration and pass it down the production chain from big media companies to publishers, artists and then to titles themselves. To be taken seriously as a scientific category, diversity would require *qualitative* indicators. But classical economics, unsuitable for this task, multiplies quantitative variables instead. And other different disciplines and traditions fail to overcome this problem: when studied in terms of diversity, cultural programs are not actually analyzed using the required categories (Magis and Perticoz 2020). This is why the notion of cultural diversity, unlike that of cultural exceptionalism, has been so easily endorsed by different (and often contradictory) theoretical discourses:

as its definition encompasses a wide range of considerations, from the normative economic regulation of cultural production to very general opinions about anthropological differences and globalization that largely exceeds the field of cultural production, its analysis is equally unclear, relying on tautological indicators. Ultimately, the problem surpasses the simple question of quantitative versus qualitative approaches. In his classic book *The Cultural Industries*, David Hesmondhalgh (2013, 271–278) shows that diversity is also very difficult to assess, even within more comprehensive approaches, less dependent on official studies and therefore on classical cultural economics. Many sociopolitical studies have been carried out on the subject, well away from the need to inform cultural policies, using textual analysis as a more precise means of analyzing diversity in music, film or journalism (with categories such as genres or formats). But the results have been contradictory even within the same corpuses, especially when trying to link the issue of diversity with that of market concentration. In each case, however, researchers seem to land on their ideological feet: advocates of the free market conclude that regulationist cultural policies tend to hinder cultural diversity, whereas defenders of tighter juridical control over cultural production observe that the latter is optimal in situations of low concentration.

For all its conceptual shortcomings, diversity is a disputed category and its appropriation by opposing theories and ideologies allows it to retain its internal contradictions: the notion aims at an ideal of democracy, even seen through the prism of media production—and even when it is not always explicit. And this (generally unsaid) normative basis allows for the continuity of critical studies on the media based on diversity and therefore their ability of claiming some publicity. Put another way, even if diversity contains a polysemy that has tempered its most critical impulses, this also implies a plurality of theoretical approaches. Hence, a discussion of the possibility of greater democracy, although marked by mediacentric determinism, remains theoretically possible using the category of diversity and creating comprehensive indicators. The fact that most theoretical discussions of diversity usually start with a critique of its methodological limits reveals that the notion's theoretical necessity also lies in the controversies it creates, probably more than in its actual scientific results. Because these controversies fundamentally rely on the idea of an ideal democratic media and cultural system:

> The ideal media system in a democracy, then, would be accessible at a variety of levels, diverse, relevant and engaging. Put another

way, the media would serve as a prime vehicle for the creation of a truly functional *public sphere*, a term coined by German philosopher Jürgen Habermas and later refined by such scholars as Nancy Fraser.

(McAllister 1996, 4)

Any agreement on such a consensual and abstract program from progressive media theorists can be criticized, even by some of their colleagues. In this respect, Nicholas Garnham argues that with such abstract Marxism, some self-proclaimed "critical" media theorists end up repeating the same "dreadly familiar" story over and over:

> The capitalist mass media are increasingly concentrated on a global scale under the control of corporations and media moguls leading to a decline in cultural diversity, the suppression of progressive political views, and the destruction of local cultures. The proposed cure for this situation is some form of regulation and/or state supported public service media and cultural production sometimes linked to appeals to grass roots activism and 'democratization'.
>
> (Garnham 2011, 42)

But whether this "dreadly familiar" story is the result of a critical decline within studies on diversity or a vague critical mantra, the fact remains that the theme of "cultural diversity" could eventually lead to more radical theoretical approaches.

Towards "discoverability": cultural platforms versus *consumed* diversity

The progressive "platformization" (Mansell 2015) of contemporary everyday life has attracted the interest of diversity theorists as cultural sectors have become entangled in the new business models typical of "platform capitalism" (Langley and Leyshon 2017). The shift towards an online platform economy has exacerbated existing problems caused by concentration and added new ones.

Although theoretical definitions of platforms vary, one of their distinctive features consists in digitally coordinating constituencies in two-sided, and often multisided, markets: they "work as mediating entities between upstream and downstream agents such as sellers and consumers" (Hoelck and Ranaivoson 2017, 19). This specificity tends to generate significant network effects as an incremental increase in the number of users on one side draws more users on the other side(s). In the digital world, these effects can be enormous. Once enabled, such effects also lead to economies of scale and successful platforms can therefore attain extremely powerful positions (Baldwin and Woodard 2009), resulting in high entry barriers (difficulty for new competitors to enter the market) and thus heightening concentration. Furthermore, these outcomes are accentuated when leading platforms strategically strengthen their position by using their power to enter new markets and push out competitors. This is how platforms from outside the cultural sector such as Amazon, Apple or Google have become major players using different strategies, such as using cultural products as integrated loss leaders to make their overall offer more appealing and to increase their grip on upstream or downstream sectors (e.g., through developing or financing of exclusive content). This tendency towards greater concentration in the digital platform economy raises questions since "strong incentives that platform networks provide for platforms to enter and possibly also leverage market power in adjoining markets, point to a reduction of innovation by third parties in the longer term" (Hoelck, Cremer and Ballon 2016), and ultimately to less diversity. But, here again, studies which assess the impact of digital platforms and of platform consolidation on diversity have drawn ambiguous and contradictory conclusions over and above the above-mentioned problems of measurement. First, since digitalization has highly reduced storage and distribution costs, every possible title becomes virtually available and, in consequence, offering the most exhaustive catalogue gives an appreciable competitive edge to most platforms (such as Netflix for visual content or Spotify for music). Consequently, supplied variety is almost total on platforms. Furthermore, this variety in the offer increases as digital services make producing and distributing content easier. Drawing on Chris Anderson's "long tail" theory (2006), according to which digital environments encourage a more diverse offer and ultimately a higher *consumed* diversity, some researchers have analyzed the positive consequences of platformization for cultural diversity (Ranaivoson 2016; Jang 2017). But analyses of platform strategies have shown otherwise (Celma and Cano 2008) and other experimental studies have revealed how the expansion of platform ecosystems ultimately tends to reduce the internal content diversity (Lee and Hwang 2018).

As mentioned earlier, these studies have generally tried to emphasize the "diversity of exposure" (i.e., the content "actually *consumed* by media users"; Napoli 2011, 246) in opposition to the diversity of production, especially in policy debates, revealing an emerging interest in "the dynamics of how media users are navigating today's increasingly fragmented media environment" (Ibid., 255). This is an important theoretical shift as it highlights consumption to the detriment of symbolic content. In terms of the indicators generally used for measuring diversity, this shift tends to accentuate the importance of *balance*: in the face of unprecedented choice due to the digitalization of content and distribution channels, do users extend their tastes? This question has especially raised interest in the recommendation systems at the core of the platformized cultural economy and in their algorithms based on close surveillance of users' digital experience. Furthermore, the interest in recommendation has grown since the electoral breakthroughs of populist political movements in Europe and the US (from 2016 onwards) and "filter bubbles" (Pariser 2011) or fake news are given as explanations for this. Regarding the question of cultural content, Neta Alexander (2016) warns that over and above the narrative of "on-demand utopia" surrounding the rise of services such as Netflix, the platform's opaque system of personalized recommendation runs the risk of imprisoning the user in an ocean of consensual and unchallenging content. Other research has aimed at categorizing recommendation systems. Two logics have emerged: collaborative filtering (where the user is recommended titles liked by people with similar tastes) and content-based filtering (where the user is recommended titles classified in the same musical categories, e.g., genres and artists, according to past behavior), most systems offering a specific combination of both. Within these categories, Robert Prey (2018) has notably focused his attention on the discovery algorithms of music platforms. The author compares the recommendation system of the Pandora Internet Radio (which uses a database called the "Music Genome Project") with that of Spotify, showing the precision of their content-based or collaborative filtering, which draws on musical "genes" in the Pandora recommendation system or on the analysis of every comment posted about a title in the case of Spotify. More importantly, these studies observe how essential recommendation systems have become for the competitivity of platforms: even when users have little or no use for it, the perceived quality of personalized recommendation is a decisive feature in their assessment of the overall quality of the offer (Seaver 2019; Bouquillion 2020).

It is in this context that recent French and Québecois studies, often commissioned by Francophone institutions, have advanced the theme of "discoverability", previously limited to information science. Whereas some research has been carried out, sometimes in association with cultural platforms such as Netflix or Spotify, to find ways of adjusting their algorithms to provide more diversity (Anderson et al. 2020), questions have arisen in the French-speaking world concerning the impact of socio-technical systems associated with online recommendations on the invisibilization of some content, notably in French. An introduction can be found in the discussions during the 2015 conference, "Diversity of Cultural Expressions in the Digital Era", held at UNESCO in Paris for the tenth anniversary of the 2005 Convention on the Protection and Promotion of the Diversity of Cultural Expressions. In some debates reported in the proceedings, the problem of algorithmic diversity turned into the question of "'discoverability', leading consumers to a wider range of cultural content" (Hanania and Norodom 2016, 618). The notion was then transposed into strategic reflections about the visibility of French-speaking content in Québec, in a context of wider English-speaking influence, and produced documents[5] and conferences such as the "Summit of Discoverability" and the "French-speaking Cultural Content Access/Discoverability" international conference held in Montréal, respectively, in May 2017 and October 2019. Through the OIF, further research on this theme has been carried out in association with French and Québec cultural institutions (Maisonneuve 2019; Roberge, Jamet, and Rousseau 2019) culminating in the Franco-Québécois Mission on the Online Discoverability of French Speaking Cultural Content (MFQ) which commissioned a report (MFQ 2020a) and published a synthesis for a common strategy (MFQ 2020b).

The category of "discoverability" does not intend to replace that of "diversity" as the latter replaced the theme of "cultural exceptionalism", but to transpose the problems of diversity in the age of platforms. As the MFQ report (2020a, 7) states "the influence of a cultural content among potential audiences relies more and more on its discoverability—and even more so when it isn't a novelty". Nevertheless, as the last section will show, considering the problem in terms of "discoverability" ultimately completes its transposition into the realm of the user practices and the human-machine interface. It is a step further towards rejecting the question of *produced* diversity in which the Francophone cultural policies also abandon the regulation of cultural content.

Semantic shifts, theoretical pragmatism and ideological changes in cultural policy

The theme of discoverability arises from legitimate questions concerning cultural life in an algorithm-driven existence. Furthermore, its promotion by international Francophone institutions puts a pragmatic emphasis on the problem: although culture in French enjoys a certain international influence, its contents are nevertheless dominated by more globally influential English-speaking programs. Reports on discoverability aim at addressing this situation with concrete propositions to remedy this situation. But behind an apparently more pragmatic and problem-solving rhetoric, the works and propositions to which the category has given rise so far seem to reproduce the errors that the theme of diversity made at the end of the 1990s, and even abandons certain pretentions that the earlier term held.

In need of a pragmatic and proactive rhetoric

First, reading the growing theoretical and institutional literature on "discoverability", one is inevitably struck by its pragmatic logic and proactive rhetoric. On the one hand, starting from the fact that the concept of discoverability is not yet well known or understood, various reports have produced sectorial data analyzing its issues among the different cultural industries. The proceedings of the 2019 Montréal conference on discoverability (Tchehouali and Agbobli 2020) give a large place to such sectorial studies, which document how cultural practices are increasingly shaped by recommendation systems; how the latter function; how they are used by different categories of people; or how issues of content visibility affect different actors. The report on the "Situation of discoverability and access to French language cultural content on internet" (hereafter EDL 2020), commissioned by the OIF, also offers an impressive theoretical inventory. However, the literature on discoverability proposes some simple advice for cultural policies, sometimes supplemented by "calls to action" to "mobilize, raise awareness and invite the various of stakeholders within the International Francophonie to assume their responsibilities and act in a concerted, consensual and coherent way in favor of greater accessibility and discoverability of French-language content in the digital environment" (Tchehouali and Agbobli 2020, 185) and to encourage more research (MFQ 2020a, 28). The general rhetoric is that of a need for change, with accents of previous "cultural exceptionalism" period with concepts such as "cultural hegemony" (EDL 2020, 43) or "cultural sovereignty" (MFQ 2020a, 36) in order to criticize, on the one hand, the platformization of the cultural economy and the consequences of opaque algorithms on users' cultural lives, and on the other, the reasons for the previous "non-mobilization" of supranational institutions (Vlassis 2020, 76). Such strong rhetoric in search of pragmatic solutions is especially active when describing the case of Québécois or French-speaking African content, generally invisible, even within the overall offer in French (EDL 2020; Jamet 2020; Thoër et al. 2020). Policies have until now been too timid, resulting in a decline of French-speaking cultural influence; it is time therefore to "reaffirm the importance of the public sector for a cultural governance capable of guaranteeing greater promotion and protection of the diversity of French-speaking cultural expression" (EDL 2020, 81).

Abandoning attempts to regulate the economic structures of platforms

If an important feature of the literature addressing issues of "discoverability" lies in its radical and proactive rhetoric in the face of "worrying issues" posed by recommendation algorithms (MFQ 2020a, 10), an examination of the various propositions ultimately reveals how limited their scope is, aiming mainly at affecting the practices of audiences, artists, cultural creators and promoters and not platforms. The general objective is better education: to "mobilize the cultural stakeholders" (MFQ 2020b, 4); to "promote the use of quality metadata" (Ibid., 5); to "gain a better understanding of content discovery processes" (Ibid., 6); or to "reinforce the digital skills of artists, professionals as well as civil organizations involved in the audience education and intercultural mediation" (EDL 2020, 81). It appears that these levers apply only to the different constituencies of the multisided markets. Some propositions do seem, however, to address the regulation of the platform economy. The first "recommendation track", in the report commissioned by the OIF, reads "Positioning French-language local/national content as niche products, through quota measures applicable to the recommendation systems of transnational platforms" (EDL 2020, 81). But further presentation shows that this measure is aimed at curators: "Producers and agents of Francophone artists must intensify their lobbying efforts and negotiations to convince platforms to integrate and exhibit their artists and titles in their playlists". Even the idea of quotas concerns the creation of "diversity playlists".

Instead of reaffirming the need to weigh collectively in favor of regulating media giants with tighter social control of algorithms at national or supranational (e.g., the EU) levels, these propositions instead aim at helping other parties to better comply with the algorithms presumed functioning.[6] In fact, by doing so, they reaffirm the platform's influence, urging French-speaking artists, especially from developing countries, to profit from the increased possibilities of exposure in the digital world (EDL 2020, 39). Yet, the platforms are also content producers or financers, and "different ways of financing and organizing cultural production have traceable consequences for the range of discourses and representations [...] and for audience access to them" (Golding and Murdock 2000, 70). By concentrating on recommendation systems, the literature on discoverability abandons any objective of platform economic regulation. At most, it advocates supporting alternative platforms (EDL 2020, 81; MFQ 2020a, 33) or "good practices" (MFQ 2020b) from traditional platforms, letting the latter know that they could attract more users by providing greater discoverability to French-speaking content. Platformization as a business model is taken for granted and postulated to be the best way of promoting diversity, even when platforms are owned by "companies or owners located outside the French-speaking linguistic space and who have no particular sensitivity that would justify their commitment to the promotion of values conveyed by cultural expression or creativity in French" (EDL 2020, 30).

The unsaid in standardization

Finally, this postulate empties cultural policy theory of an important political element: the issue of cultural standardization. As we have seen, this issue was considerably diminished in the shift from "cultural exceptionalism" or the critical concepts of early theoretical works to "diversity". But in the debates surrounding measurement as well as in the underlying rhetoric of democracy seen through the complexity of its constitutive cultural indicators, especially that of "disparity", the theme of diversity contains a potential critique of the cultural limitations of democracy. In comparison, even when relating the theme of discoverability to that of diversity, discussions about the former rapidly disregard the question of the latter's measurement. They usually note the difference between produced and consumed diversity and emphasize the latter, pointing out that a plethoric offer of online international cultural content tends to disadvantage local products (EDL 2020, 32). Hence, most empirical research carried out on discoverability has focused on simpler socioeconomic indicators to assess users' online behavior (Jamet 2020; Thoër et al. 2020) or the functioning of recommendation systems. The report commissioned by OIF has, for example, signed up on the music streaming platform Deezer in order to observe the performance of recommended titles each day and comparing it to the general presence of content in French (EDL 2020). In this report, even when conducting research with multiple facets (analysis of recommendation systems, users' strategies, etc.), the indicators in each domain are ultimately reduced to a sole variable and the different indicators are not linked. Tchehouali's report for Patrimoine Canada (Tchehouali 2020) advances three criteria for characterizing discoverability: "locationability" (*repérabilité*), "predictability" and "recommendability". Yet these categories are less intended for measurement as much as they function as slogans to help French-speaking cultural producers gain visibility on the platforms. Some reports do not even intend to measure discoverability, and refer to other reports and studies (MFQ 2020a). So far, discoverability measurement is scarce and somewhat secondary in current discussions, and one cannot help but think that paradoxically the general question of democracy, even seen in terms of the vitality of cultural production, is left aside.

Ultimately, discussion tends to imply that content in French escapes any suspicion of standardization *by design*. This tendency is probably caused by the fact that the literature on discoverability stems from Francophone institutions which aim at promoting French-speaking content. But by equating discoverability of content in French with the influence of a so-called "French-speaking culture" (Briceño 2020, 25), convinced in advance of the richness of the latter (EDL 2020, 7) and of the openness of French-speaking users (Ibid., 65), the problems posed in terms of discoverability finally seem to forget that the language of a cultural item or of its producers does not save it from standardization. Furthermore, it obliterates the fact that content in French can be produced by global media majors, sometimes in association with French-speaking companies, but that does not mean promotion of what the reports vaguely term "French-speaking culture" and "representation".

Conclusion

The domains of cultural theory, and of cultural policy, like the cultural industries they survey, document, and regulate are fond of novelties. Their history is thus one of terminological changes and semantic shifts. But such shifts also have political resonances. This chapter has analyzed how the movement away from earlier critical studies of the global cultural economy and their incorporation in cultural policies has produced the "weak" concept of "diversity" (A. Mattelart 2005). But in the reports commissioned by Francophone organizations, the newer theme of "discoverability", although intending to offer pragmatic solutions to specific issues of diversity in a language that sometimes recalls the most critical impulses of "cultural exceptionalism", runs the risk of a shift towards an even weaker concept. Though this theme is not intended to replace that of diversity, the pragmatic nature of its proposals, its lesser pretension to regulate media giants and its intense promotion by leading cultural institutions is likely to encourage this semantic shift. To counter this, further discussion on discoverability should aim at questioning its ambitions. Since its emergence occurs within a set of legitimate political and economic issues concerning cultural life in the digital world, the scope of its "calls to action" should primarily involve intervention at these political and economic levels.

Notes

1 « Netflix Europa », *The Economist*, Apr. 3rd 2021, p. 24.
2 A study by D. Fuchs and Klingemann (2011) observes that « cultural diversity » is an important constituent of the European identity.
3 The "General Agreement for Tariffs and Trade" is a treaty initially signed in 1947 by 23 countries which agreed to harmonize their customs policies in order to reduce or eliminate trade barriers. It was replaced by the WTO in 1995, after agreement by 123 nations.
4 "Remark by Vivendi Chief Unnerves French Film Industry", *The New York Times*, Dec. 24, 2001.
5 In 2016, the Québécois office for French language created a terminological entry for the term, defining it in the following terms : "The potential for an online available content to be easily discovered by Internet users in the cyberspace, especially by those who were not specifically looking for it", see http://gdt.oqlf.gouv.qc.ca/ficheOqlf.aspx?Id_Fiche=26541675; the MFQ report (2020a, 5) offers a somewhat similar definition: "the online availability and ability of content to be spotted among a vast array of other content, especially by someone not specifically looking for it".
6 Initiatives such as the "Découvrathon", launched in the wake of these propositions, is thus a general call for projects likely to better integrate programs in French in the algorithm. See https://www.decouvrabilite-francophonie.net/decouvrathon/

Bibliography

Alexander, Neta. 2016. "Catered to Your Future Self: Neflix's 'Predictive Personalization' and the Mathematization of Taste." In *The Netflix Effect: Technology and Entertainment in the 21st Century*, edited by K McDonald and D. Smith-Roswey, 81–97. New York, NY: Bloomsbury.
Anderson, Chris. 2006. *The Long Tail: Why the Future of Business Is Selling Less of More*. New York, NY: Hyperion.
Anderson, Ashton, Lucas Maystre, Ian Anderson, Rishabh Mehrotra, and Mounia Lalmas. 2020. "Algorithmic Effects on the Diversity of Consumption on Spotify." In *Proceedings of The Web Conference 2020*, 2155–2165. New York, NY, USA: Association for Computing Machinery. https://doi.org/10.1145/3366423.3380281.

Baldwin, Carliss Y., and Jason Woodard. 2009. "The Architecture of Platforms: A Unified View." In *Platforms, Markets and Innovation*, edited by Annabelle Gawer, 19–44. Cheltenham: Edward Elgar.

Benhamou, Françoise. 2006. *Les Dérèglements de l'exception Culturelle*. Paris: Seuil.

Bouquillion, Philippe. 2008. *Les Industries de La Culture et de La Communication : Les Stratégies Du Capitalisme*. Grenoble: PUG.

———. 2020. "Les Stratégies de Visibilité, Le Rôle Des Plateformes." *Enjeux Numériques* 10: 21–26.

Bourreau, Marc, François Moreau, and Pierre Senellart. 2011. "La Diversité Culturelle Dans La Musique Enregistrée En France (2003–2008)." *Culture Études* 5: 1–16.

Briceño, Catalina. 2020. "La Découvrabilité : Fer de Lance d'une Présence Numérique Durable Pour Le Patrimoine Audiovisuel Francophone Canadien." In *Accessibilité et Découvrabilité Des Contenus Culturels Francophones.../ Regards Croisés...*, edited by Destiny Tchehouali and Christian Agbobli, 21–30. Villiers St-Josse: HDiffusion.

Burri, Mira. 2015. "The European Union, the World Trade Organization and Cultural Diversity." In *Cultural Governance and the European Union*, edited by Evangalia Psychogiopoulou, 195–209. Basingstoke, Hampshire: Palgrave Macmillian.

Celma, Oscar and Pedro Cano. 2008. "From Hits to Niches? Or How Popular Artists Can Bias Music Recommendation and Discovery." In *NETFLIX '08: Proceedings of the 2nd KDD Workshop on Large-Scale Recommender Systems and the Netflix Prize Competition*, Article No. 5, 1–8. https://doi.org/10.1145/1722149.1722154

Downing, John D. H. 2011. "Media Ownership, Concentration, and Control. The Evolution of Debate." In *The Handbook of Political Economy of Communications*, edited by Janet Wasko, Graham Murdock, and Helena Sousa, 140–168. Chichester: Wiley Blackwell.

Doyle, Gillian. 2002. *Understanding Media Economics*. London & New-York, NY: SAGE.

Emmanuel, Aghiri. 1972. *Unequal Exchange. A Study of the Imperialism of Trade*. New York, NY: Modern Reader.

Fuchs, Dieter, and Hanns-Dieter Klingemann, ed. 2011. *Cultural Diversity, European Identity and the Legitimacy of the EU*. Cheltenham: Edward Elgar.

Garnham, Nicholas. 2011. "Political Economy of Communication Revisited." In *The Handbook of Political Economy of Communications*, edited by Janet Wasko, Graham Murdock, and Helena Sousa, 41–61. Chichester: Wiley Blackwell.

Golding, Peter, and Graham Murdock. 2000. "Culture, Communications and Political Economy." *Mass Media and Society* 3: 70–92.

Greffe, Xavier, ed. 2006. *Création et Diversitéa Au Miroir Des Industries Culturelles—Actes Des Journées d'économie de La Culture*. Paris: La Documentation française.

Hamelink, Cees J. 1983. *Cultural Autonomy in Global Communications. Planning National Information Policy*. New York, NY: Longman.

Hanania, Lilian Richieri, and Anne-Thida Norodom, eds. 2016. *Diversity of Cultural Expressions in the Digital Era.* Paris: Teseo.

Hesmondhalgh, David. 2013. *The Cultural Industries.* London: Sage.

Hirsch, Paul M. 1972. "Processing Fads and Fashions: An Organization-Set Analysis of Cultural Industy Systems." *American Journal of Sociology* 77: 639–659.

Hoelck, Katharina, Stefan Cremer, and Pieter Ballon. 2016. "Cross-Platform Effects: Towards a Measure for Platform Integration Benefit", paper presented at *the 14th International Open and User Innovation Society Conference (OUI)*, Harvard, Boston, MA, USA. https://ssrn.com/abstract=2817994

Hoelck, Katharina, and Heritiana Ranaivoson. 2017. "Threat or Opportunity? Cultural Diversity in the Era of Digital Platforms in the EU." *Quaderns Del CAC XX* 43: 17–28.

Jamet, Romuald. 2020. "L'impact Social Des Algorithmes de Recommandation Sur La Découverte Des Contenus Musicaux Francophones Québécois." In *Accessibilité et Découvrabilité Des Contenus Culturels Francophones.../ Regards Croisés...*, edited by Destiny Tchehouali and Christian Agbobli, 53–69. Villiers St-Josse: HDiffusion.

Jang, Sunjin. 2017. "Cultural brokerage and creative performance in multicultural teams." *Organization Science* 28 (6): 993–1009.

Langley, Paul, and Andrew Leyshon. 2017. "Platform Capitalism: The Intermediation and Capitalization of Digital Economic Circulation." *Finance and Society* 3 (1): 11–31. https://doi.org/10.2218/finsoc.v3i1.1936.

Lee, Changjun, and Junseok Hwang. 2018. "The Influence of Giant Platform on Content Diversity." *Technological Forecasting and Social Change* 136: 157–165. https://doi.org/10.1016/j.techfore.2016.11.029.

Magis, Christophe. 2020. "Political Economy of Communication: The Critical Analysis of the Media's Economic Structures." In *Reimagining Communication: Meaning*, edited by Michael Filimowicz and Veronika Tzankova, 197–212. London and New York, NY: Routledge.

Magis, Christophe, and Lucien Perticoz. 2020. "La musique comme analyseur : mutations de la filière musicale et mutation de la recherche sur la musique." *Tic&société* 14 (1–2): 13–65. https://doi.org/10.4000/ticetsociete.4666.

Maisonneuve, Sophie. 2019. "L'économie de la découverte musicale à l'ère numérique." *Reseaux* 213 (1): 49–81.

Mansell, Robin. 2015. "Platforms of Power." *Intermedia* 43 (1): 20–24.

Mattelart, Armand. 1976. *Multinationales et Systèmes de Communication. Les Appareils Idéologiques de l'impérialisme.* Paris: Anthropos.

———. 2005. *Diversité Culturelle et Mondialisation.* Paris: La Découverte.

Mattelart, Armand, Xavier Delcourt, and Michèle Mattelart. 1984. *International Image Markets: In Search of an Alternative Perspective.* London: Comedia Publishing Group.

Mattelart, Tristan. 2008. "Globalization Theories and Media Internationalization. A Critical Appraisal." In *Internationalizing Media Studies*, edited by Daya Kishan Thussu, 48–60. London and New York, NY: Routledge.

————. 2011. "La 'Diversité Culturelle' : Quelques Éléments de Déconstruction Théorique." In *Diversité et Industries Culturelles*, edited by Philippe Bouquillion and Yolande Combès, 23–37. Paris: l'Harmattan.

McAllister, Matthew. 1996. *The Commercialization of American Culture*. London: Sage.

McChesney, Robert W. 2008. *The Political Economy of Media: Enduring Issues, Emerging Dilemmas*. New-York, NY: Monthly Review Press.

Moreau, François, and Stéphanie Peltier. 2004. "Cultural Diversity in the Movie Industry: A Cross-National Study." *Journal of Media Economics* 17 (2): 123–143.

Musitelli, Jean. 2006. "The Convention on Cultural Diversity: Anatomy of a Diplomatic Success Story." https://www.diplomatie.gouv.fr/IMG/pdf/The_Convention_on_Cultural_Diversity.pdf

Napoli, Philip M. 2011. "Exposure Diversity Reconsidered." *Journal of Information Policy* 1: 246–259.

Nordenstreng, Kaarle, and Herbert I. Schiller, eds. 1979. *National Sovereignty and International Communication*. Norwood, NJ: Ablex.

Nordenstreng, Kaarle, and Tapio Väris. 1974. "Television Traffic – A One-Way Street? A Survey and Analysis of the International Flow of Television Programme Material." Paris: Unesco.

Pariser, Eli. 2011. *The Filter Bubble: What the Internet Is Hiding from You*. New York, NY: Penguin.

Pool, Ithiel de Sola. 1977. "The Changing Flow of Television." *Journal of Communication* 27 (2): 139–149.

Prey, Robert. 2018. "Nothing Personal: Algorithmic Individuation on Music Streaming Platforms." *Media, Culture and Society* 40 (7): 1086–1100.

Ranaivoson, Heritiana. 2016. "The Internet Platforms' Impact on the Diversity of Cultural Expressions: to the Long Tail, and Beyond!". In *Diversity of Cultural Expressions in the Digital Era*, edited by Lilian Richieri Hanania and Anne-Thida Norodom, 237–263. Paris: Teseo.

————. 2019. "Online Platforms and Cultural Diversity in the Audiovisual Sectors: A Combined Look at Concentration and Algorithms." In *Audio-Visual Industries and Diversity: Economics and Policies in the Digital Era*, edited by Luis Albornoz and Trinidad Garcia Leiva, 100–118. New York, NY: Routledge.

Rao, C. Radhakrishna. 1982. "Diversity and Dissimilarity Coefficients: A Unified Approach." *Theoretical Population Biology* 21 (1): 24–43. https://doi.org/10.1016/0040-5809(82)90004-1.

Roberge, Jonathan, Romuald Jamet, and Andréanne Rousseau. 2019. *L'impact Social Des Algorithmes de Recommandation Sur La Curation Des Contenus Musicaux Francophones Au Québec. Enquête Qualitative*. Québec: Institut national de la recherche scientifique.

Schiller, Herbert I. 1970. *Mass Communications and American Empire*. New York, NY: Augustus M. Kelley.

————. 1976. *Communication and Cultural Domination*. New-York, NY: Sharp.

Seaver, Nick. 2019. "Captivating Algorithms: Recommender Systems as Traps." *Journal of Material Culture* 24 (4): 421–436.

Stirling, Andrew. 1998. "On the Economics and Analysis of Diversity." *SPRU Electronic Working Paper*, no. 28.

Tchehouali, Destiny, and Christian Agbobli, eds. 2020. *Accessibilité et Découvrabilité Des Contenus Culturels Francophones…/ Regards Croisés…* Villiers St-Josse: HDiffusion.

Thoër, Christine, Christian Agbobli, Florence Millerand, and Destiny Tchehouali. 2020. "Prendre En Compte Les Usagers Des Plateformes Dans La Découvrabilité Des Séries : Expériences de Jeunes Adultes Au Québec." In *Accessibilité et Découvrabilité Des Contenus Culturels Francophones…/ Regards Croisés…*, edited by Destiny Tchehouali and Christian Agbobli, 31–43. Villiers St-Josse: HDiffusion.

Vlassis, Antonios. 2020. "Gouvernance Mondiale de La Culture et Découvrabilité Culturelle à l'ère Numérique : La Francophonie, Un Acteur International Incontournable?" In *Accessibilité et Découvrabilité Des Contenus Culturels Francophones…/ Regards Croisés…*, edited by Destiny Tchehouali and Christian Agbobli, 73–81. Villiers St-Josse: HDiffusion.

Reports

EDL, 2020: État des lieux de la découvrabilité et de l'accès aux contenus culturels francophones sur internet, Villiers St-Josse: HDiffusion.

MFQ, 2020a: Mission Franco-Québécoise sur la découvrabilité en ligne des contenus culturels francophones, Rapport, Ministère de la Culture et des Communications du Québec et Ministère de la Culture de France.

MFQ, 2020b: Mission Franco-Québécoise sur la découvrabilité en ligne des contenus culturels francophones, Stratégie commune, Ministère de la Culture et des Communications du Québec et Ministère de la Culture de France.

Tchehouali, Destiny. 2020. "Diversité Des Contenus à l'ère Numérique : Analyse Des Mesures Potentielles En Appui à l'accès et La Découvrabilité Du Contenu Local et National." Patrimoine Canada.

2 Modern Mathemagics

Values and Biases in Tech Culture

Jakob Svensson

Introduction

It is March 2019, and I am attending the legendary tech, innovation, music, film, and comedy festival South by Southwest (SXSW2019). In one panel on Artificial Intelligence (AI), a panelist states that users in front of the screens think of AI as magic. The panelists seem to agree that AI is just statistics, "just really advanced mathematics." But must magic and mathematics be in opposition to each other? The following day, I listen to Cassie Kozyrkov, head of Decision Intelligence at Google. This is the first time I hear the term *mathemagics*. Like the panelists the day before, Kozyrkov highlights the danger when tech users in front of the screen mystify what goes on behind it. While I agree with her, this is not the main reason I become intrigued by the concept. For me, the seemingly unlikely marriage of mathematics and magic is a perfect description of tech culture, its role in contemporary connected societies, and the perception of digital technology by users in front of the screen as well as programmers behind it. (I use programmers as an umbrella term for software developers, engineers, and designers behind the screen.) The magic of tech consists of programming languages: binary machine code of ones and zeroes that search and find hidden patterns in so-called big data and perform tricks such as explaining and predicting future behavior. Thus, it seems that the magic of tech is not any kind of magic; it is mathematical magic. This is the magic of science in combination with fiction, of being creative and artistic and thinking outside of the famous box while still adhering to rationality and the logics of numbers. Mathemagics is an excellent concept that gets to the heart of tech culture and programming with all its allure, biases, and contradictions.

I am not the first scholar to link magic and tech. For example, Nagy et al. (2020) studied time management technologies as "magic bullets"

DOI: 10.4324/9781003173373-2

that help users become more organized and efficient and remarked on how these are sold as time-saving miracle devices. Frosh (2019) described tagging pictures on Facebook as technological feats of magic, connecting names to mediated bodies (images) with the aim of animating digital social networks. Frosh connected this to the ancient magical power of *incantation*: the use of words to perform actions at a distance. The articulation of a name makes images of the named materialize instantly before others.

The first day I set foot in a tech conference, I felt like I had entered an enchanted world with sagas and colorful unicorns. Magic was mentioned throughout many of the talks. For instance, Chris Dancy stated in his presentation that any sufficiently advanced technology is indistinguishable from magic (referring to Science Fiction author Arthur C. Clarke). To further link technology with the magical, he argued that wireless charging is another word for energy projection and voice interface can be compared to casting spells. I managed to catch Chris after his talk. "I see myself as a magician," he exclaimed, and he insisted that technology could be used for good things, so "don't unplug," which is also the title of his at the time newly released book (Dancy, 2018). At the conference, he had set up a booth that reads *Phone Palmistry—free reading*. Like a fortune-teller at a village fair, Chris retold my past, present, and future. However, instead of looking at my hand, he looked at my smartphone home screen.

It is easy to draw parallels between magicians and programmers. Like magicians on stage, programmers perform tricks with their programming skills in mind-blowing demonstrations of new digital devices. (Just think about Steve Jobs introducing new Apple products in his so-called Stevenotes.) They predict the future, control the world, and disrupt it with their knowledge of code and mastery of programming languages. The programmer becomes someone who stands between us in the physical world and a virtual world of code and data. Because of their knowledge of this other world, they can make things happen in this world. Like wizards, they imagine the impossible and bring out the magic that is believed to be harbored in computers (see also Svensson, 2021).

In connected societies, we are increasingly dependent on algorithms, automated systems, and digital technology in most walks of life. In other words, we become dependent on the programmers' imaginations that lie behind the technologies we use. However, programmers are not your average Joe (or average Svensson as we say in Sweden). They are predominately white, male, and young, which leads to biases in the systems and devices they develop (as I have discussed elsewhere; see Klinger & Svensson, 2021; Rosales & Svensson, 2021).

Digital technologies embody rules, ideals, imaginations, and perceptions. They are encoded with intentions that may or may not be fulfilled. Therefore, a study of the humans and culture behind them is pivotal if we intend to have an informed discussion of algorithmic biases and shifting relations of power in contemporary connected societies. Mansell (2012) has particularly underlined the role of imaginaries (i.e., deeper normative notions and images) and their impact on how the technologies are used, how they permeate and mediate people's lives, and how they shape the technologies themselves. In a similar vein, Bucher (2017) has argued that what she labels as "algorithmic imaginaries" are productive (pp. 40–41). Digital technologies are thus outcomes of humans' imaginaries. Following this, when I later map the magic in tech, I will attend to (1) how technologies are described and (2) how programmers present themselves. First, I will offer some notes on a growing disenchantment of tech, which forms a backdrop against which I seek to discuss the magic metaphor in tech.

The evil side of mathemagics

Given programmers' increasing power, it is surprising how little tech users know about them and the imaginations behind the systems and devices they develop. This is a one-way mirror formed by a fundamental lack of transparency, as Pasquale (2015) argued in his book *The Black Box Society*. Therefore, algorithms and automated systems are difficult to hold accountable. A well-known example is Google's image-search algorithm: A search for *three white teenagers* resulted in a multitude of (for sale) stock photography, while a search for *three black teenagers* resulted in mug shots. Consequently, Google was accused of being racist. Google's algorithm was created by humans working in a for-profit organization geared towards connecting sellers and buyers of stock photography, a majority of whom are white. Nonetheless, at one point Google claimed that even if the algorithm was racist (or its results), this could not be blamed on Google. However, as Noble (2018) argued in her book *Algorithms of Oppression*, with the telling subtitle *How Search Engines Reinforce Racism*, it is the combination of private interests in promoting certain sites and the monopoly status of a relatively small number of search engines that leads to biased search algorithms that privilege whiteness and discriminate against people of color. Indeed, as technology is designed and engineered by humans, it operates with biases just like the rest of society. This is a powerful argument for why it is important to study the programmers involved in the making of digital technologies and automated systems.

There is a growing awareness of these inbuilt biases. Scandals such as the Facebook-Cambridge Analytica, where the firm browsed millions of Facebook profiles and used their data without consent for political purposes in elections, have increased concerns around surveillance and data protection. There is an increasing discomfort around the use of AI-powered automated systems in, for example, predictive policing, university ranking, job application, credit, and insurance worthiness. O'Neill (2016) showed how predictive policing systems in the US send cops back to the same poor neighborhoods, creating a toxic feedback loop because policing one street creates new data that justifies more policing in that exact same street. Since every police arrest creates more data, Latinos and blacks become more likely to be stopped in crime prevention measures. As Eubanks (2017) underlined, while people in connected societies live under this new regime of data and automated systems, the most invasive and punitive systems zoom in on the poor.

Indeed, mathemagics can become evil, as theologian and philosopher Giordano Bruno (1548–1600) underlined already in the 16th century. Bruno was arguably the first to think about mathematics as magic. For Bruno, there are three sorts of magic: divine magic, natural magic, and mathematic magic (see Gosnell's 2018 translation). Bruno associated three different kinds of worlds to his three different types of magic. For divine magic, there is the archetypal world; for natural magic, the physical; and for mathematical magic, not surprisingly, the rational world. When it comes to mathematical magic, Bruno argued that this is a magic that locks the world, and things in this world, in symbolic meanings, "symbols that mean something" (Gosnell, 2018, p. 15). According to Bruno, making sense of symbols requires imagination rather than physical senses. In other words, mathematics becomes an imagination that interacts with people and has bearing in this world people inhabit.

Bruno warned against a possible "evil side" of mathematical magic. According to him, it is important to avoid trying to capture or fix it into rigid categories and regularities, accepting that there will always be things that are unknown. Evil mathemagics happens when spells, rituals, and practices become locked into fixed manuals. It is easy to draw parallels to O'Neill (2016) and the perils of predictive policing. A smoke screen of mathematical symbols in societies with a "pervasive desire for numbers" (Kennedy, 2016) gives an allure of objectivity, neutrality, and fairness. Consequently, when mathemagics is directed at us, it tends to be unquestioned. According to O'Neill (2016), such smoke screens are why predictive policing is believed to be scientific, fair, and largely accepted when it is in fact biased. Numbers and data have an allure of objectivity and neutrality, a higher and more scientific knowledge, and thus may appear as magic for tech users.

Those who are too focused on rules and regularities and governed by mechanical thinking and logical rigidity, Bruno labels such persons as "pedants" (cited in Bornemark, 2018, p. 47). One example of such pedantry is when Bob Saunders (a famous hacker) declined his wife's request to help her bring in the groceries. She phrased it as a question, whether he "would like to help" her. When the wife got mad at Bob, he allegedly answered, "I don't like to, but if you ask me to help, I do it" (cited in Levy, 1984, pp. 25–26). Indeed, for spells to work correctly, they need to be uttered in an exact manner, following a precise order; otherwise, the computer (or the hacker) will not understand.

The rigidity argument has also been made by more contemporary scholars. For example, Peters (2015) criticized written languages for their fixity. Once something is inscribed, it becomes fixed and "all the spontaneity, mobility, improvisation, the quick responsiveness of spoken speech vanishes" (Peters, 2015, p. 305). As Peters explained, when spoken, *but* and *butt* sound the same. It is the context that makes people understand their different meanings. In written languages, we try to replace the specificity of circumstances with letters and signs, but then we end up with a mode of communication which can only deal with predefined/pre-calculated differences. Programming languages are written languages and hence fixed. In programming languages, following mathematical Boolean logic, everything can be reduced to binary code—truth and falsehoods, ones and zeroes. Nuances get lost and unintentional consequences become difficult to handle.

To discuss the evil side of mathemagics, namely biases in tech, we therefore need to consider both the programmers (those developing the systems, platforms, and devices we are so dependent on in contemporary connected societies) and the tools they use (i.e., programming languages). This leads me to the empirical data that underpins the argument in this chapter.

Empirical data

Empirically, this chapter is based on a two-and-a-half-year research project in which I interviewed programmers and made observations in various tech conferences, tech headquarters (when conducting interviews), and meetups. I have also conducted an in-depth study of the process of introducing and implementing a particular algorithm in a particular setting: an algorithm to rank and mix news on the front page of a Scandinavian newspaper. In this chapter, I will discuss only the parts of the material that connect to magic.

For the interview study, I adopted a mixed recruiting strategy: snow-balling personal contacts and approaching programmers through the platforms LinkedIn and Meetup. Both are popular in the programming community. A LinkedIn premium account allowed me to filter programmers based on their location and work tasks. For example, before going to Silicon Valley, I used the search function to find programmers working at the big social media companies in the Bay Area. In total, I conducted 39 interviews in Brazil, Denmark, Germany, India, Sweden, and the US with programmers originally from Brazil, China, Denmark, Estonia, Germany, India, Israel, Lithuania, Mexico, the Netherlands, Poland, Sweden, and the US. The interviews were conducted from 2018 to 2020 and the interviewees consist of freelance programmers, in-house programmers at the newspaper, and programmers from smaller startups to tech giants. Most of the interview participants (31 of the 39) identified themselves as men. The youngest participants were in their early 20s and the oldest in their 50s.

Apart from interviews, I have also attended conferences and meet-ups in Austin, Bangalore, Berlin, Chennai, Copenhagen, Malmö, Sao Paulo, Silicon Valley, and Stockholm. Meetup is a service used to organize online groups that host in-person events for people with similar interests. The platform allows you to search for events concerning a particular topic (such as coding) within a distance you set yourself from a location. I used Meetups to find events to participate in and observe and to find interviewees. I also wanted to target certain groups, such as women who code in Silicon Valley, to diversify my sample. Hence, the sample cannot be claimed to be representative of the programming community at large. In total, I attended 20 meetups. Further, I conducted observations at four tech conferences, the afore-mentioned newspaper, five workplaces, and two startups.

By observing tech conferences and talking to programmers, I aimed to paint a rather broad picture of people who have an increasing amount of power in contemporary connected societies. A limitation of this is that details as well as contradictions tend to end up in the background. While tech culture and programmers are generally quite homogeneous, there are still differences between coders, developers, and project owners. Freelance programmers do not have exactly the same motivations as big tech employees, and programmers from India are not identical to programmers from Germany. However, the focus in this chapter is on the broader picture.

Throughout my data gathering, I was open about who I am and the purpose of my research. Apart from Chris Dancy (who is a public figure), the participants have been anonymized as much as possible. I explained this "middle-masking" (Kozinets, 2011) to all participants and secured informed consent. I also signed a confidentiality agreement with the newspaper, which prevents me from revealing the name of the newspaper and any kind of information that concerns their business model. However, someone familiar with the Scandinavian news ecology might be able to figure out which newspaper I studied.

Mapping the magic in tech

Having briefly accounted for the methods employed and the empirical data, I now turn to the systematic mapping of the magic metaphor in my empirical material. In this section, I will first present this mapping, which I have divided into two categories: magic in descriptions of digital technology and magic in programmers' own self-presentations. Then I will connect the magic in tech to modernity.

Magic in the way digital technology is described

Digital technology and devices are often described as magic. This is especially apparent in hacking. In his book about hackers, Levy (1984) stated, "the computer is a magic box, it's a tool, it's an art form … the ultimate martial art" (p. 189). Levy (1984) wrote about the aura of mysticism that surrounds the world of technology and hacking and how computer science should rather be called witchcraft. Years later, Rosenberg (2008, p. 15) followed a software team for three years and concluded that their symbols and metaphors have a layer of magic and mythopoetic heroism to them. An example is how things are named, such as using Avalon (the mystic place of King Arthur; see Rosenberg, 2008, p. 169). Another interesting example here is General Magic, the former legendary American software company based in Silicon Valley that preceded Apple to create handheld gadgets. Fisher's (2018) chapter on General Magic is full of pocket crystals, pixie dust, supernatural links, and magic machines. This equation of computing with magic is reinforced when I visited the Computer History Museum in Mountain View in March 2019. Before entering the museum, visitors are met by a huge sign with the following inscription: *Those living before us would call it magic. But it's not magic it is software.*

One of the most prominent magic symbols I have come across during my journey into tech is the unicorn, used in everything from names of tech startups that are valued at $1 billion or more to symbols of tech organizations attempting to make the world a better place. Indeed, the unicorn connotes something that is rare and magical; it is a symbol of hope and purity as well as strangeness. The meaning of the unicorn as a symbol has shifted over time and in different places. During the Middle Ages and the Renaissance, the unicorn was simultaneously described as a wild creature of the woods and a symbol of purity and grace (see Svensson, 2021). Unicorns became allied with reports of exotic creatures and had a reputation of being elusive—things that could neither be seen nor be caught. Strong and powerful yet pure and graceful, this resembles how programmers in my interviews described code or "elegant code" to be precise. For example, I asked Pelle in Stockholm what he meant by elegant code:

PELLE: Elegant code is simple code, simple but beautiful, yet does what you expect of it, if not more. It is strong as other programmers will understand it and use it in their programs.

JAKOB: Beautiful?

PELLE: Yeah, you just get it immediately by looking at the code. It is not banal. There is not a lot of extra lines just to explain the functions. The labels are smart, to the point, and yeah … you just get it.

Indeed, computers and code open the door to another world, as is apparent in the many virtual reality (VR) and augmented reality (AR) demo stations set up in the open spaces of conference venues I have attended. Attendants always seemed eager to try them out. The look on their faces showed how amazed they were by these applications and what they can do. Talking to conference attendants about their fascination, I heard about a general disenchantment with the so-called "real" world. That the real world has shortcomings, and that this world is possible to transcend through technology, is illustrated in an interview with Roger, who works at Google. He argued that through technology and through understanding how the brain works, it was possible to "detach yourself from humanity and some of the shortcomings of being human."

What is the function of magic here? My interviews revealed that this is not evil or black magic. Rather, magic here is about attending to shortcomings of the "real" world and helping users in front of the screens by first imagining solutions and then solving all kinds of problems through mastering programming (see also Svensson, 2021). For example, Bart, a Dutch programmer I interviewed in Copenhagen, stated that he "would like to develop code that actually does something in the real world." This was exemplified in the interview:

BART: What software can do in the *real world*, especially when you connect it to devices, like this device [points at his Google watch] or have a sensor or something, that is awesome, incredible. It is just so cool that you can just write some text on an editor and then *press a button and then … bam, something that actually does something in the real world.* That *magic* I am still very impressed by. And it is still *magic* to me. (Emphasis added)

Conceiving of magic as means for solving problems, helping users with their problems, and making the "real" world a better place resonates with the wizard label, which is common in tech. For example, General Magic's version of the iPhone, the one that came 14 years before the iPhone, was called "sharp Wizard." People at General Magic were perceived as wizards (Fisher, 2018, p. 306). The term "wizard" was also used for a set-up assistant that started with the 1991 launch of Microsoft Publisher. As it was targeted at nonprofessionals, Publisher's "Page Wizards" provided a set of forms to produce a complete document layout. The wizard is also a theme that resounds in programmers' self-presentations, which leads me to the next section.

Magic in the way programmers present themselves

Magic is all over the statements of Silicon Valley pioneers in Fisher's (2018) interview book *Valley of Genius*, in which programmers claim to do magic and create magical devices. Further, hackers have presented themselves as magicians for a long time. Thomas (2002) wrote that hackers have become the new magicians as they master the machines that control modern life. To simply click and command has become the equivalent of using spells or a magic wand. Instead of spells, programmers use code. Just add some lines of code and "the program will do all the things you wanted it to do" (Rosenberg, 2008, p. 2). Levy (1984) similarly talked about hackers making the computer do what they wanted it to do, "like Aladdin's lamp, you could get it do your biddings" (p. 34). Thus, hackers conceive of themselves as having this ability to make the seemingly impossible a reality through their skills in computing. The idea of complex technology "exoticizes computer hackers, making them seem increasingly mysterious and capable of almost superhuman hacking feats" (Thomas, 2002, p. 154).

This notion of mastery was a prevalent theme in the interviews. For instance, Roger at Google described how he as a kid, when first encountering computers through his mum, fell in love with programming because he could tell the machine what to do and then it would do it: "I felt I could do whatever I wanted, with whatever outcome, if I just thought long enough about the input." Sören, a senior programmer at Microsoft, described his role at work as "the one who decides what our programs can do, what you can do with them, and how they work."

It is programming languages that programmers need to master. Bring the magic out of computers and into the world requires knowledge of programming languages: "If one character, one pause, of the *incantation* is not strictly in proper form, the magic doesn't work" (Brooks, 1975, p. 8, emphasis added). Programming languages are thus used as magical spells on the machine. Data in different combinations are the ingredients, the herbs, wizards use in their magic brews and elixirs. Programming languages are what they use for their spells, their very own *abracadabra*. Chun (2008) has written about this as "sourcery," combining the words "source code" and "sorcery." Chun (2008) argued that the invisibility, ubiquity, and alleged power of source code lend itself nicely to an analogy with the magical. Furthermore, she claims that source code is "a medium in its full sense of the word as it channels the ghost that we imagine runs the machine" (Chun, 2008, p. 310). Just like magical spells, programming languages act in this world without most users really understanding how. Thus, mastering programming languages becomes equivalent to using spells.

Connected to the idea of magic as mastery of programming languages is the idea of magic as based on programmers' imagination. Knowing what is possible to do with code influences programmers' imagination and vice versa; beyond craftsmanship lies imagination (Brooks, 1975). The possibilities of what *could* be done with programming languages seem not to be the main problem. Imagination is what is needed. For example, Bart underlined that people are "not imaginative enough yet to actually figure out what we can do with it." Indeed, bringing out the magic in the machine demands its wizards, the ones that use their imaginations in connection with their knowledge of programming languages (spells) to make this world a better place. In an interview in Malmö with Andri, I asked him what the biggest problem was with computers today in terms of what he thought they should do that they did not do. He answered that the potential of computers is bigger than people's ability to use them:

JAKOB: So, what is the problem, that we don't pose the right questions to the computer or some kind of lack of imagination, or?
ANDRI: I think there are several aspects. First of all, there are quite many people who don't know what they could do with computers so … applying computers in various areas that aren't connected to information technology right now, such as better food services, industrializing music, and stuff like that … that is probably

ignorance, that *people don't know that they could do with computers*, or perhaps lack of resources, time, and imagination. (Emphasis added)

The ability to envision things has always been a wizardry characteristic. The programmer seems to be someone who has visions of the future, who knows how to solve problems and how things should work, and who makes this happen. In this sense, imagination precedes mastery of programming languages. Before programmers can create something new, they need to imagine it: "I saw the potential of what a machine could do; I saw all these possibilities," Gabriela in Sao Paulo phrased it. At Facebook headquarters, Martin praised Facebook CEO Mark Zuckerberg as "a great visionary." Nadja in Silicon Valley talked about one of her role models as someone who was "just an amazing visionary." Programmers indeed value visionaries.

Wizards are also common in programmers' self-presentations. I first came across this in a meetup called "Wizard Amigos." In Malmö, when answering my question on how he would describe his profession, Hans stated, "I say I am like a wizard; I make the things appear on the computer that you want to appear." In the preface to Levy's (1984) *Hackers*, the list of characters in the book has the title "Who's Who: The Wizards and Their Machines" (p. xi).

As discussed previously, the wizard label implies a helpful attitude. This resonated in almost all my interviews. "We are a tech team that helps others," Anders, a programmer at the newspaper, described himself and his team of programmers. Python in Berlin stated, "I don't want to sell people stuff they don't really need; I want to help, solve problems." This was further underlined in the interview with Bart when I asked about his heroes and role models. He mentioned Bill Gates because he was "changing the world for the better," trying to cure HIV/AIDS and malaria. In the interview with Martin at Facebook, he proudly proclaimed that his technology helped in the fight against amyotrophic lateral sclerosis (ALS) and made the world a better place: "We helped others, and that was very rewarding."

Modern mathemagics

This mapping of the use of magic in tech suggests a belief in tech as something that will make our world better in the future. For this to happen, programmers need to master programming languages—hence their self-presentations as wizards, as persons who help users with their problems. Magic here signals the possibility of the impossible, of solving all kinds of problems. Accordingly, connotations to magic in tech underline that the physical, "real" world has shortcomings but that these can be addressed through programming languages on big sets of data—a magical dimension built upon binary code of ones and zeroes. Like spells, programming languages bring the genie out of the bottle and make the physical, "real" world a better place in the future.

Many scholars have made an analogy between tech and religion (see Bogost, 2015; Peters, 2015). However, magic and religion are not the same. Whereas religion requires people to change their lives and obey a higher authority, magic underlines manipulation as a way to change people's lives, the lives of others, and the world around (Fortea, 2014). Whereas religion requires faith, worship, and obedience, magic is the quest to control forces of nature yourself. Within religion, one prays to a God and asks for his/her good will. In magic, people have a possibility to change circumstances themselves, through manipulation, through access to something hidden and secret—through access to programming languages. However, before using their skills to manipulate the physical world into a better place, they need to imagine this improved world. We rely not only on programmers' knowledge of programming languages but also on their imagination, how they envision a better world.

Manipulation and control in the quest for a better future (i.e., progress) are themes that resonate in modernity. According to Weizenbaum (1976, p. 126), it was the quest *to control* the power manifested in the computer that drew programmers to the machine in the first place. Further, Wiener (1948, p. 37) argued that the thought of every age is reflected in its technology and that computers are all about communication and control. Seventy years later, Whittaker (2018) continued to argue that contemporary digital technologies are instruments of management and control. Nagy et al. (2020) discussed time-hacking technologies as an opportunity to orchestrate life trajectories to use tech to *control* mental and biological pasts, presents, and futures.

Revisiting the interviews, I found that being in control is pivotal. When I asked the programmers to look back on why they became interested in computing, the moment they realized that they were in control, could master the computer, seemed defining. Pedro, a Mexican programmer in Austin, emphasized that the computer was a screen that he could control, and this was what drew him into programming. All the other screens up to that point in his life did things he had no control over, but the computer was different: "I remember like I felt I controlled the TV." Mark in San Francisco similarly referred to control when explaining why he got into programming (via computer gaming):

MARK: I had this world that I had complete control over; it was a world I could master, and I felt like it was possible for me to understand the whole thing and that there was nothing unpredictable about it.

Wanting to be in control through magic resonates in science fiction novels. In his classic *Neuromancer*, Gibson (1984) talked about console cowboys, data jockeys who could manipulate the system towards their own gains. Thus, magic is simultaneously about empowerment and an acknowledgment that we live in a scary, an unknowable world, which creates an impulse to try to control life itself and the future.

Other researchers have also made the connection between digital technology and modernity. Rosenberg (2013) associated the rise of the concept of data to modernity, and Jarzombek (2016) argued that data processing is about making the self and others predictable, identifiable, and exploitable as in the directive of modernity. Participation in the project of modernity has always meant that one becomes "a calculable subject" (Raley, 2013, p. 126). Further, Kunda (2006) discussed how tech is presented as having a mission, namely to forward progress and individualism. People work in tech "in the name of humanism, Enlightenment and progress" (Kunda, 2006, p. 225). Indeed, modern beliefs in endless progress lurk behind these optimistic ideas of a better future through technology.

Another theme that resonates in both tech and modernity is the embrace of (organic) disembodiment. It was the search for a human essence, detached from the physical body, that led to the notion of an immortal soul in religious thinking. The body is flesh and is associated with sin and will eventually die. The soul, however, is spiritual and connected to higher life-forms and will live on forever. In modernity, Descartes (2017/1647) gave scientific sanction to this body/soul dualism by reframing it as a body/mind split. He argued that the mind is the seat of intelligence, not the physical brain; the mind takes precedence over the body. Therefore, it is possible to trace ideas of creating superhuman intelligence (see Bostrom, 2014) to older assumptions inherited from modernity that humans may be reduced to their minds. To make the body obsolete would be the ultimate (magic) trick of modernity.

I have encountered imaginations of upgrading, or getting rid of, the physical body all over tech culture. Hackers have always had a problematic relation to the body. In popular depictions, hackers are overweight and unattractive, spending long hours in front of a computer and neglecting their bodies, but behind the computer, they are omnipotent (Thomas, 2002, p. 192). According to Levy (1984, p. 163), programming is the ultimate disembodied activity. To enter cyberspace, you need to forsake your own body and become information. This is about tech opening doors to another magical world in which decaying bodies are irrelevant. This theme also resonates in science fiction novels. For example, *Neuromancer* protagonist Henry Dorsett Case jacks himself "into a custom cyberspace deck that projected his disembodied consciousness into the consensual hallucination that was the matrix" (Gibson, 1984, p. 6).

At the same time, to marry magic to modernity is not easy. In modernity, magic implies a violation of the idea that the world can be accurately described in terms of mathematical laws and thus be controlled (Bornemark, 2018, p. 235). This idea is at the heart of magic in tech. Mathemagics is the magic of mathematical laws (binary code) in combination with imaginaries of a better world possible to achieve through programmers' imaginations and knowledge of programming languages. However, these modern aspects of control through a rigid mathematical Boolean logic are behind the growing disenchantment of tech- and AI-powered automated systems and their previously discussed biases.

Conclusion and outlook

This chapter aimed to understand tech culture, its values, and its biases through the metaphor of magic. It concludes that magic signals the possibility of the impossible, the possibility of solving all kinds of problems and challenges we face in the "real" world. With the help of programming languages making calculations on big sets of data, our world will become a better place in the future. For this, we rely on programmers and their skills and imaginations. However, programmers and the cultures they act in and through are neither objective nor neutral. Hence, the products, platforms, and services they develop will have biases. Therefore, it is important to also ensure satisfactory representation in terms of whose imaginations are listened to and considered. Further, it is not likely that the power of data, algorithms, and automated systems will diminish any time soon. It is thus pivotal to bring in more perspectives and more imaginations to seriously address the issue of biases in tech. Since imaginaries are never settled and always up for negotiations (Mansell, 2012, p. 5), we should enable more people from different backgrounds and age groups to participate in imagining what problems technology should address and how. Technology is too important to outsource to only one group of people. Also because imaginations are about power—in this case, the power to shape algorithmic calculations, automated systems, and AIs that will act upon us humans in this world we inhabit.

Moreover, there are problems and practices that are *not* suitable for tech solutions. I agree with Pasquale's (2015) argument that it is possible to imagine a future in which the power of algorithms and automated systems are limited to environments where they *may* promote fairness and freedom. As Weizenbaum (1976) explained, the question is not so much a matter of what computers *could* do but what they *should* do. This is where tech could become magical in a positive way, considering different kinds of possibilities while at the same time retaining a critical mindset and not resorting to the pitfalls of so-called *technological solutionism*. Morozov (2013) complained that tech's desire to solve all kinds of problems, its will to improve, is shortsighted because it recasts complex situations as neatly defined tech problems with computable solutions. He particularly argued that politics is one area that should be left untouched by technological solutions.

Technological solutionism is championed not only by programmers themselves, but tech users also resort to this. It is arguably tech solutionist imaginaries that provide people in front of the screen the distorted view of technology that Kozyrkov complained about (in this chapter's introduction). Indeed, user's imaginations, that is, their projections onto tech and programmers, are also important to study. For example, Bucher (2017) showed how users' imaginaries are important for, in her case, the molding of the Facebook algorithm itself. Accordingly, digital technologies are not only outcomes of programmers' imaginaries. How people imagine the internet frames their understanding of it (Mansell, 2012). Hence, a call for attending to the humans behind digital technology would also entail a focus on tech users' imaginations.

When it comes to outside users' projections onto programmers and digital technology, my empirical material only allowed me to access these through the accounts of the programmers themselves as well as from the accounts of the editors and journalists interviewed in connection to the study of the newspaper. Nevertheless, outsiders evidently also approached programmers as wizards. Through their skills in computing, programmers are thought capable of helping users to solve all kinds of problems in more or less magical ways. Nagy et al. (2020) referred to tech as "a magical panacea" for all problems in almost all walks of life. Comor and Compton (2015) labeled the belief in digital technology to magically solve all problems as "technological fetish." It is when technology is fetishized that programmers are transformed into wizards—people who make the impossible possible. Tech is the magic trick that makes a problem disappear or become solved. Technological solutionism is thus connected to magic, through the image of a programmer waving his magic wand and uttering some spells in precise programming language.

While flattering for the programmers, this image could also create problems. For example, Ted, an app programmer in Malmö, complained over customers that come in and ask for an app and the price without any idea of what it should do and what data it should be based on. He was asked to program an app that solves a problem without the problem being properly defined by the customer. In the study of the newspaper, the in-house programmers were interested in journalism and had some kind of basic understanding of the profession. However, it was not always the other way around. The programmers I interviewed felt that journalists underestimated how difficult it was to program certain functions. Journalists treated their in-house programmers as wizards that could just cast a spell of code and the functions journalists wished for would magically appear. One of the programmers illustrated this by mimicking a journalist: "There should be a button there, and when you press the button, it should bring up exactly the stuff you like." This was further exemplified in an interview with another programmer at the newspaper:

DANIEL: If someone who is *not* technically knowledgeable should think about a solution that … "there should be a button there, and when you press the button, it should bring up exactly the stuff you like" [mimicking a journalist]. … and then you are like … from where does the stuff you like come? And he answers, "from pressing the button" … but if there was a button that selects articles you like, then there must be a model behind it, some really advanced AI. (Emphasis in original)

While sometimes annoying for programmers, this fetishization of technology has its benefits and feeds into programmers' own previously discussed identification. That many outsiders perceive of technology as alien, unfriendly, and hard to understand resonated in the programmers' self-image as geniuses, doing extremely complicated stuff. "Not even my wife understands," Sören at Microsoft stated, "you know, it is a little bit abstract."

Therefore, we need to stop fetishizing technology and to ensure there is enough diversity among those imagining what tech could do or should do. It is indeed possible to make our future world magic again. First, modernity needs to be left behind, or at least the modern view of magic that currently dominates tech where everything can be fixed and reduced to mathematical laws and regularities. For Bruno, the universe is living and thinking, and this is what makes it magical. He specifically underlined the importance of accounting for "all the miraculous things that are in nature" (cited in Gosnell, 2018, p. 14), and perhaps also the magic within people themselves. If we lose ourselves in rules and regulations, we also lose contact with the specificity of our circumstances—the magic of the different situations we find ourselves in. Bruno's teachings can thus be applied to contemporary connected societies and used for a normative argument against the rigidity of computers and for rehumanizing automation. Bruno attempts to make the world magic again through presenting the nature around us as well as ourselves as living and unpredictable beings. This is the magic of the uniqueness in specific situations, of the unpredictability of the present moment, of being around other unpredictable humans. This is about allowing magic to happen to us and within us.

References

Bogost I (2015) The Cathedral of Computation. We're not living in an algorithmic culture so much as a computational theocracy. *The Atlantic*, 15 January.

Bornemark J (2018) *Det omätbaras renässans. En uppgörelse med pedanternas herravälde*. Stockholm: Volante.

Bostrom N (2014) *Superintelligence: Paths, Dangers, Strategies*. Oxford: Oxford University Press.

Brooks F (1975) *The Mythical Man-Month: Essays on Software Engineering*. Boston: Addison-Wesley.

Bucher T (2017) The algorithmic imaginary: Exploring the ordinary affects of Facebook algorithms. *Information, Communication & Society*, 20(1): 30–44.

Chun WHK (2008) On "Sourcery," or code as Fetisch. *Configurations*, 16(3): 299–324.

Comor E and Compton JR (2015) Journalistic labour and technological fetischism. *The Political Economy of Communication*, 3(2): 74–87.

Dancy C (2018) *Don't Unplug. How Technology Saved My Life and Can Save Yours Too*. New York: St. Martin's Press.

Descartes R (2017) *Meditations on First Philosophy, with Selections from the Objections and Replies*. In: Cottingham J (ed) Cambridge: Cambridge University Press. First published 1647.

Eubanks V (2017) *Automating Inequality. How High-tech Tools Profile, Police and Punish the Poor*. New York: St. Martin's Press.

Fisher A (2018) *Valley of Genius*. New York: Hachette Book Group.

Fortea JA (2014) What is the difference between magic and religion? In: Spiritual Direction. Available at: https://spiritualdirection.com/2014/04/03/difference-between-magic-religion (accessed 20 November 2019).

Frosh P (2019) You have been tagged: Magical incantations, digital incarnations and extended selves. In: Lagerkvist A (ed) *Digital Existence. Ontology, Ethics and Transcendence in Digital Culture*. New York: Routledge, pp. 117–136.

Gibson W (1984) *Neuromancer*. New York: Penguin Random House.

Gosnell S (2018) *On Magic (Giordano Bruno Collected Works)*. Columbus. Windcastle Press.

Jarzombek M (2016) *Digital Stockholm Syndrome in the Post-Ontological Age*. Minneapolis: University of Minnesota Press.

Kennedy H (2016) *Post, Mine, Repeat. Social Media Data Mining Becomes Ordinary*. London: Palgrave Macmillan.

Klinger U and Svensson J (2021) The power of code: Women and the making of the digital world. *Information, Communication & Society*. Published online Aug 7, 2021 DOI: 10.1080/1369118X.2021.1962947

Kozinets RV (2011) *Netnografi*. Lund: Studentlitteratur.

Kunda G (2006) *Engineering Culture, Control and Commitment in a High-Tech Corporation*. Philadelphia: Temple University Press.

Levy S (1984) *Hackers: Heroes of the Computer Revolution*. Sebastopol: O'Reilly Media.

Mansell R (2012) *Imaginging the Internet. Communication, Innovation and Governance*. Oxford: Oxford University Press.

Morosov E (2013) *To Save Everything, Click Here. The Folly of Technological Solutionism*. New York: PublicAffairs.

Nagy P, Eschrich J and Finn E (2020) Time hacking: How technologies mediate time. *Information, Communication & Society*. Epub ahead of print 5 May 2020.

Noble SU (2018) *Algorithms of Oppression. How Search Engines Reinforce Racism*. New York: New York University Press.

O'Neill C (2016) *Weapons of Math Destruction*. New York: Crown Publishing.

Pasquale F (2015) *The Black Box Society. The Secret Algorithms That Control Money and Information*. Cambridge: Harvard University Press.

Peters JD (2015) *The Marvelous Clouds. Toward a Philosophy of Elemental Media*. Chicago: Chicago University Press.

Raley R (2013) Dataveillance and countervailance. In: Gitelman L (ed) *Raw Data Is an Oxymoron*. Cambridge: MIT Press, pp. 121–145.

Rosales A and Svensson J (2021) Ageism in the tech industry. Stereotypes and discrimination in a distinctly youth-oriented culture. *NORDICOM Review*, 42(1): 79–91.

Rosenberg S (2008) *Dreaming in Code: Two Dozen Programmers, Three Years, 4,732 Bugs, and one Quest for Transcendent Software*. New York: Crown Publishing.

Rosenberg D (2013) Data before the Fact. In: Gitelman L (ed) *Raw Data Is an Oxymoron*. Cambridge: MIT Press, pp. 15–40.

Svensson J (2021) *Wizards of the Web: An Outsider's Journey into Tech Culture, Programming and Mathemagics*. Göteborg: Nordicom.

Thomas D (2002) *Hacker Culture*. Minneapolis: University of Minnesota Press.

Weizenbaum J (1976) *Computer Power and Human Reason. From Judgement to Calculation*. New York: W.H. Freeman & Company.

Whittaker X (2018) There is only one thing in life worse than being watched and that is not being watched: Digital data analytics and the reorganization of newspaper production. In: Moore P, Upchurch M and Whittaker X (eds) *Humans and Machines at Work*. London: Palgrave Macmillan, pp. 73–99.

Wiener N (1948) *Cybernetics, or Control and Communication in the Animal and the Machine*. Cambridge: MIT Press.

3 Reading the Cards

Critical Chatbots, Tarot and Drawing as an Epistemological Repositioning to Defend against the Neoliberal Structures of Art Education

Eleanor Dare and Dylan Yamada-Rice

Introduction

Fleming (2021) writes that there is a "strong link between the neoliberalisation of Higher Education (HE) and the psychological hell now endured by its staff...academia once the best job in the world -one that fosters autonomy, craft, intrinsic job satisfaction... you would be hard-pressed to find a lecturer who believes that now" (blurb). In this chapter, we pick up on this sentiment in relation to the use of psychometric and behavioural evaluation algorithms within HE to show how this is just one example of how autonomy, craft and thus job satisfaction are being pushed out of the academy.

Explicitly psychometric algorithms, as well as less overt approaches to "personality" metrics, remote proctoring and classroom behaviour are now widely deployed in work and education. Indeed, the Cambridge Analytica scandal of 2018 centered around the apparent use of the so-called "Big Five" personality traits harvested from 87 million Facebook users. Despite their prevalence in corporate, carceral (see Benjamin, 2019; Browne, 2015) and educational contexts, psychometric approaches have long been contested with many categorising them as a pseudo-science (Murphy Paul, 2010). Hollway (1984) identified psychometric testing as a "technology of the social", representing "relations between power and knowledge" (p. 26). She went on to write how such testing is based on a reductionist dualism between society and individuals, in which "one effect of that power of psychology is to privilege the individual as the focus of activities which are in fact specific characteristics of corporate organisations" (ibid., p. 56). Likewise, remote proctoring software (technology which monitors students and claims to identify "cheating" behaviours via biometric

DOI: 10.4324/9781003173373-3

facial recognition (FR), room scanning and blocking of access to web pages) has been widely reported as discriminatory, modelling an ideal of bodily behaviour which excludes in relation to ethnicity, gender, disability and class. This reinforces the ideology of those who have originated such software, establishing a dominant and narrow model of normality.

In light of ongoing calls to acknowledge the systemic nature of social inequality, racism and misogyny and their entanglement with racist and sexist artificial intelligence (AI) systems, it is clear that such technologies are irreconcilable with social justice and their presentation as offering more equitable selection processes, wholly lacking in credibility. Furthermore, their emphasis on the individual, always constructed as separate from others (ridiculous if we consider that most scholarly activities are not carried out alone), reinforces a neoliberal ontology, one in which the possibility of addressing systemic discrimination and systemic privilege is negated. Neoliberalism has been framed as:

> ...the defining political economic paradigm of our time- it refers to the policies and processes whereby a relative handful of private interests are permitted to control as much as possible of social life in order to maximize their personal profit.
>
> (Chomsky, 1999, p. 7)

This includes the manufacture and sale of surveillant and discriminatory psychometric software, only holding back when public pressure outweighs profit.

Even Amazon has apparently identified the discriminatory nature of its own AI-driven applicant selection algorithm. In 2018, it was 'widely reported to have scrapped its own system, because it showed bias against female applicants. The Reuters news agency said that Amazon's AI system had "taught itself that male candidates were preferable" because they more often had greater tech industry experience on their resume' (Murad, 2020, n.p).

In our lived experience as academics, and despite these historical critiques, it has come to our attention how prevalent psychometric and behavioural evaluation is in HE, often remediated through automated, algorithmic processes provided by commercial platforms (an example of which is discussed in detail later). With the onset of proctoring technologies, such surveillance is now pervasive and these questionable constructs now deeply embedded within the everyday practices of universities, negatively impacting both staff and students. Since the declared moratorium on FR in 2020 by Amazon and apparent support for further caution by IBM and Google, the potential harm of AI-driven systems has now become much more widely debated, if not fully understood (see, Johnson, 2020). At the same time, the resurgence of systems which claim to generate actionable insights into human emotion, personality and behaviour has, if anything, intensified during the Covid pandemic. The move to online examination and staff candidate selection has seen AI-driven proctoring, algorithmic examination and staff candidate selection becoming pervasive. In August 2020, "A" Level school students (18-year-olds) in the UK successfully demonstrated about the unfair results generated by algorithmic exam prediction. Academics (including the authors) are currently bombarded by sales pitches for AI candidate selection and automated marking systems.

As universities moved rapidly en masse at the start of the Covid-19 pandemic, so apparently did the impetus to algorithmically monitor and by implication model the actions, intentions and emotions of online students. Even though intelligence and emotion are both contested subjects, technologies that claim to detect them, proliferate in the case of emotion, 'despite the continuing proliferation of books, journals, conferences, and theories on the subject of "emotion," there is still no consensus on the meaning of this term. Some even believe that it should be thrown out of psychology altogether' (Dixon, 2012). Illouz (2007) writes, "far from being pre-social or pre-cultural, emotions are cultural meanings and social relationships that are inseparably compressed together" (Illouz, 2007, p. 95,). When AI systems claim to detect emotions, they are detecting that which is "organized hierarchically' and that which, in turn, 'implicitly organizes moral and social arrangements" (ibid., p. 122).

Such analysis and contestation does not stem the tide of systems designed to extract an instrumentally useful construct of emotion and sentiment, one which is individualised (neoliberalised) yet unsituated, whether it is through emoticons or the complex algorithms deployed in systems such as ClassDojo, a school-based "behaviour management" technology, actively "used in 95% of all K-8 schools in the U.S. and 180 countries. 1 in 6 U.S. families with a child under 14 use ClassDojo every day. Fifteen million children have learned about Growth Mindset and Empathy with ClassDojo" (classdojo.com, n.p). Amazon Web Services offer an array of AI-driven speech analysis systems for education, for example, Oleeo.com claims to use AI to "debias" application processes. It is hard to know which services are used by HE, but the authors have "stumbled" upon dashboards for systems such as Oleeo. com by mistyping university intranet addresses for which they have access. AI-driven applicant selection systems are far from straightforward; Ruha Benjamin writes of connections between:

> the cultural power we grant to algorithms with a longer genealogy of symbols and sorcery, arguing that "computation casts a cultural shadow that is informed by this long tradition of magical thinking." Magical for employers, perhaps, looking to streamline the gruelling work of recruitment, but a curse for many job seekers.
>
> (Benjamin, 2019, p. 141)

We are aware of universities piloting AI-driven student candidate selection systems and we believe those systems (such as SpeechX) have the potential to discriminate based on accent (which is what they are designed to do), the connection between language proficiency and accent clearly has many other intersectional aspects, such as class, region, ethnicity and gender implications, opening the door for discrimination, racism, transphobia, class and disability discrimination.

What follows is an analysis of how psychometric and behavioural testing has entered the domain of HE recruitment and how it has gained a new lease of life via its rebranding as a form of AI-driven insight, often cynically associated with "diversity" initiatives and with a neoliberal construct of empathy. Empathy in this context is sociopathic, precluding systemic redress for discrimination and educational assessment gaps, as discussed within this text. The chapter also offers readers a sample of questions with which they might evaluate their own comprehension of psychometric testing. Critical chatbots and tarot, ergodic processes are presented as alternative methodologies, ones in which subjectivity and categorisation are always unstable and situated. The term ergodic is used by Aarseth (1997) to imply narratives in which the reader must work to find a path, in which "nontrivial effort is required to allow the reader to traverse the text" (p. 1–2). The word ergodic is a combination of the Greek words for work and path, which implies a high degree of agency for those who interact with such systems. We propose similarly agential approaches, ones which place agency in the hands of students and staff as a counter to the contested neoliberal ontology of desirable behaviour, emotion and aptitude.

The remainder of this chapter is structured first to provide an overview of the literature in relation to the use of psychometric testing and occupational assessment. We then go on to critique this literature further by comparing AI to a critical chatbot and psychometric testing to a tarot reading. In the final section, we suggest that art practice, specifically drawing, can provide an antidote to the harm caused by AI and psychometric testing. The work we use in these sections is auto-ethnographical and we invite the reader to see how it relates to their own experiences.

The coldest of intimacies: HE, business and psychometric/proctoring surveillance

The belief in a core, rational and "true" self, and with it, a desirable set of behaviours and traits, is arguably modelled to reflect the interests and values of those who hold power, apparently predicated "on a naïve scientific realism, in which the psychometrician presumes that his or her quantification corresponds to some underlying thing, which exists unmediated in nature, simply waiting to be measured" (Ferraro, 2014, n.p). Hollway (1984) asks this question of occupational assessment and readers might want to ask them of their own experiences:

> Does it work? The question immediately begs two others. First, what is 'it'? Second, what constitutes 'working'? In answer to the first question, it can be recognised more readily that psychological assessment is not a homogeneous body of knowledge when we see it as a production in various diverse sites.
>
> (Hollway, 1984, p. 27)

Hollway (1984) frames the conception of the individual within occupational assessment as a "social technology enabling the administration and regulation of employees" (p. 28). Within institutional assessment practices, it is naïve, in her terms, to look for a straightforward "progress towards truth" (ibid., p. 27). Hollway (1984) emphasises the historical motivation within what was then called occupational psychology, to aid organisations with "the complex problems of maximizing profitability" (ibid., p. 29). It is important to note the connections between personal psychology and commercial interests, and here, to make overt the connections between psychological assessment methodologies and the marketisation of HE trait-oriented tests, such as Costa and McRae's (2006) version of the Big Five Test of Personality, or Hans Eysenck's (1947) Big Three Supertraits, which are all predicated on more or less monolithic notions of personality traits such as extraversion-introversion, neuroticism and psychoticism.

In 1955, the personality theorist George Kelly wrote: "the aspirations of the scientist are essentially the aspirations of all men" (p. 43). Kelly's approach is a precursor to cognitive theories of personality, in which an individual's social-cognitive style or adaptation is the key to assessing their individual psychology. It is an approach that is close to the information processing paradigms critiqued by Hayles (1999), Haraway (1991), Barad (2007) and Benjamin (2019). Additionally, in framing "all men" as tantamount to the idealised figure of "the scientist", it is important to ask what types of knowledge and what types of men or indeed what types of people this statement rejects. It is also important to remember, as Henriques et al. (1984) state, that Personal Construct Theory does not take account of the Experimenter Effect, in which the experimenter's own feelings, attitudes or expectations change the outcome, nor does it take any account of wider constructs of rationality beyond Neo-Platonic idealisations. Personal Construct Theory ignores inconvenient or messy variables that are not reconcilable with a narrow conception of rationality or of rational subjects. Most significantly, Personal Construct Theory is based on a conception of the rational and unitary individual, who may be influenced by social forces or social contexts but is nevertheless distinct and separate from their society. Despite the repeated failures and flaws of these systems, HE continues to rely on models of personality traits and normative behaviour which discriminate, and exclude, reproducing discrimination and reenforcing the status quo. For example, remote proctoring aims to confirm "a student's identity and monitors him/her through a webcam. The video recorded during a remote proctored exam helps to flag any suspicious activity or behaviour" (proctortrack.com, 2020). This particular proctoring company site goes on to declare:

> Both the public and private sectors widely use online remote proctoring. More than 500 universities in the US consider remote proctoring as a viable option. Consequently, schools and colleges switch to user-friendly technologies for conducting online exams. Due to this, remote proctoring is gaining favourable momentum in the global educational sector.
>
> (proctortrack.com, 2020, n.p.)

Perhaps it is not surprising that no mention is made of the discriminatory impact of this technology beyond a nod towards the danger of discomfort or intrusion which can be addressed, they claim, by acclimatizing students to being proctored. But FR can proactively harm those who are subjected to it due to:

> ...an overreliance on standardized visual cues of engagement— precisely the kinds of indicators FR depends on—can be

ineffective or even detrimental, and there is further evidence that excessive surveillance can erode the environment of trust and co-operation that is crucial to healthy learning environments and positive student outcomes.

(Demetriades et al., 2020, n.p)

The language used on sites which advertise remote proctoring technologies is of "integrity", "personalized learning", "suspicious activities" and of being "cheat-proof". These words characterise students as transgressive, as opponents who must be surveilled and caught in the act of cheating. In turn, the kind of learning implicated in such transgression is predicated on a banking model of knowledge, in which facts are poured into students and reproduced without recourse to such disobedient strategies as reading a website; it implies a reversion to rote learning by drilling facts into students, it is conservative and regressive in its conception of how learning takes place, taking us back to a 19th-century model of passive learners with miscreant subjectivities. What these systems proctor is a social order, a form of capitalism that according to Illouz (2007):

went hand in hand with the making of an intensely specialised emotional culture and that when we focus on this dimension of capitalism – on its emotions so to speak – we may be in a position to uncover another order in the social organization of capitalism.

(p. 122)

Swauger (2020) reports on the extremely negative impact on students of remote proctoring technologies, describing how:

a Black woman at my university once told me that whenever she used Proctorio's test proctoring software, it always prompted her to shine more light on her face. The software couldn't validate her identity and she was denied access to tests so often that she had to go to her professor to make other arrangements. Her white peers never had this problem.

(n.p.)

While students with children or disabilities were similarly discriminated against by the proctoring technologies, "several proctoring programs will flag noises in the room or anyone who leaves the camera's view as nefarious. That means students with medical conditions who must use the bathroom or administer medication frequently would be considered similarly suspect" (ibid., n.p). Trans-students also experience being "flagged up" by proctoring technologies, which are predicated on a narrowly normative modelling of what a body should or should not look like during an exam. Despite the negative impact, the use of such technologies is on the increase and unlikely to be abated, as neoliberal governments push to keep courses online or blended after the pandemic. Why, we might ask, do HE and other organisations persist with technologies which are rife with controversy? Demetriades et al. suggest it is because these "increasingly sophisticated tools offer a veneer of control and efficiency in their promise to pluck individuals out of a mass of data and assign categories of identity, behaviour, and risk" (2020, n.p.), but even more significantly, universities:

> bear significant power to influence our collective future through the students they prepare, the insights they generate, and the way they behave. In light of this unique dual role of both academic and civic leadership, we must begin by recognizing the reality of deeply rooted systemic racism and injustice that are exacerbated by surveillance technologies.
>
> (Demetriades et al., 2020, n.p)

Psychometric evaluation of job applicants in HE is similarly driven by a desire to spot those with undesirable traits as well as recruiting those who match an institutionalised construct of appropriate personality. This is despite the fact that even some of the companies who developed such technologies have admitted their faults:

> VIA – an American psychology organisation – recently admitted that their personality test is a failure and told a UK government agency to stop using it on jobseekers. After flunking its scientific validation, the test was discredited and put out of use. To reiterate, this was a test being used by an official UK government agency.
>
> (Abercombie, 2015, n.p)

Braidotti (2002) is energetic in the call for "more innovative and creative energy in thinking about the structures of subjectivity at a time in history when social, economic, cultural and symbolic regimes of representation are changing very fast" (p. 73). But Braidotti also asks, is the:

> model of scientific rationality a suitable frame of reference to express the new subjectivity? Is the model of artistic creativity any

better? How does it act upon the social imaginary? Will mythos or logos prove to be a better ally in the big leap across the post-modern void?

(ibid., p. 173)

It is interesting to note that a writer who so keenly identifies the dangers of either/or thinking should create, albeit rhetorically, an opposition between scientists and artists, as if art and science are binary constructs and as if art can represent everyone any more than science can. Writers such as Braidotti (2002), Alcoff and Potter (1993), Hollway (1984) and Ansari (2020) have cogently argued that Western notions of the subject have been predicated upon universalising and damaging sets of dualisms, and in doing so, these dualisms have shaped almost every aspect of Western culture, establishing entrenched, polarised forms of knowledge production. Foremost in the oppositions established by a Western conception of the subject are the separations between body and mind and between the individual and their society.

The following two sections critique these technologies. First, in relation to AI by reflecting on Dare's work developing critical chatbots which attempt to deconstruct Cartesian dualism while critiquing the idea of personality types. Second, through comparing the results of a psychometric test administered as part of an academic job application against a tarot reading of the same questions.

Flawed chatbots surface the absurdity of AI-driven psychometric systems

At this point the file of cards was again connected with The Devil, already set in that place by the previous narrator.

(Calvino, 1977, p. 23)

Dare's work with chatbots and AI-driven psychometric systems started in 2005; with an Expert System for matching readers to books, the system deployed rudimentary psychometrics, generative of absurdity and misunderstanding. This work was further developed as part of her PhD in Arts and Computational Technology (2007–2011), culminating in a critical psychometric system for exploring constructs or AI and subjectivity. Postdoctoral work by Dare continues to explore the limits of such systems as well as their absurdity and entanglement with discriminatory models of normative subjects. In this work, humour is deployed as an embodied presence, reminding us of that which disembodied, un-situated AI can replicate but cannot grasp. According to Stengers (2015), humour does not have to be:

> ...merely the guardrail of scientific passions. It can be the constitutive condition of these passions. And this will be the case if demands are invented where scientists could become the "measure" of becomings that do not authorize the separation between the production of knowledge and the production of existence.
>
> (Stengers, 2015, p. 166)

Dare's chatbot called Lent was developed over three years, from 2007 to 2011, and was framed as both a character and a surveillant worker which had spent its (or "his") working life immersed in the raw material of CCTV footage, extrapolating meaning from it – forensic, psychometric and epistemic. Lent's obsession with creating an ontology of digital vision and subjective insight was chaotic and often contradictory, enabling something akin to what Stengers (2015) articulates as the 'humour that would permit us to treat the avatars of our belief in the truth as contingent processes, open to a reinvention with "other givens," it seems to me, is vital for resisting the shame of the present' (Stengers, 2015, p. 164). The shame of the present is colonial domination, discrimination and social injustice; our work critiquing psychometrics and proctoring is committed to both surfacing the ways in which that injustice is embedded in technologies (reflecting the ideologies of its makers), but also in formulating different ways of being and of recognising myriad subjectivities.

Stengers (2015) writes that both "the strength and the weakness of statistics reside in what they show and what they ignore" (p. 7). Dare's chatbot Lent cannot grasp subjectivity, emotions or personality traits beyond the rote learnt human patterns Dare gave the program, including data scrapped from the Web. The chatbot character Lent is both a software agent and the fictional protagonist of a book and website called "Road", which could be described as an agent-based psychometric text adventure in both of its forms. Lent is not a helpful agent in the sense evoked by Maes (1994), but a troublesome servant with his own needs that are not always congruent with those of his "masters" or readers. Lent is arguably closer to an unidealised human servant as opposed to an idealised software servant or agent entity who would follow orders without complaint, conflict or fatigue. He is also closer to the notion of a believable agent as defined by Mateas (1997), one that has a rich personality and social interactions that are consistent with his character, motivations and goals. Mateas is keen to emphasise that believable agents are not to be confused with truth-telling, functional agents such as those who filter us for job applications or spot us "cheating" in exams:

For many people, the phrase believable agent conjures up some notion of an agent that tells the truth or an agent you can trust. But this is not what is meant at all. Believable is a term coming from the character arts. A believable character is one who seems lifelike, whose actions make sense, who allows you to suspend disbelief. This is not the same thing as realism (Mateas, 1997). Lent was created in response to the failings of Dare's work with a purely Eliza-style agent, the main technical frame of reference in attempting to construct a more stimulating, less deterministic character, and to test if it could generate insights into humans. To paraphrase Russell and Norvig (2002), Lent makes his decisions based on the things he believes in and the things that he wants (p. 584). Unfortunately for his readers, the thing Lent wants most in the world is alcohol. Lent's dependence on alcohol (purely algorithmic, of course) creates an immediate point of tension with his readers, who initially perceive him as a helper agent in the vein of Microsoft's paperclip, "Clippy" or "Office Assistant". Readers are led to believe that Lent is this type of helper agent, one who can provide information and advice while they try to navigate the virtual world of the interface. Though Lent is an extremely simple agent, Dare differentiates "'him" from an even simpler reactive agent (which reacts in a way that is almost reflexive to its environment), in that Lent maintains an internal state relating to "his" levels of alcohol consumption. Lent is consistent with the requirements for a deliberative agent and with Wooldridge's (2009) requirements for an intelligent agent, in that "he" or it is:

- Situated – "he" is embedded in an environment.
- Goal directed – "he" has goals that "he" tries to achieve.
- Reactive – "he" reacts to changes in "his" environment.
- Social – "he" can communicate with other agents (including humans).

Lent believes he needs alcohol; this is different from the knowledge base that was embedded in the Expert System that Dare used for an earlier psychometric project, in that Lent's beliefs are subjective and do not have to be "true", accurate, helpful or immutable. Lent also believes in a lot of information about South London. However, Lent's desires or motivations are conflicted; he "wants" to talk to readers in a way that usefully conveys the information he knows, but he also

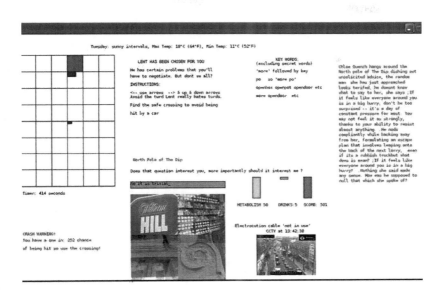

Figure 3.1 A screenshot from 'Road' a deliberative agent interface that uses expressive text-to-speech (Dare, 2007–2011).

"desires" alcohol and is motivated by the desire to steer his readers towards the pub, where he can top up his alcohol levels (as indicated by the central bar chart in Lent's interface; see Figure 3.1). The more Lent drinks, the less coherent he becomes, the less servile and arguably the less useful as an indentured digital servant. However, the less he drinks, the more forceful he becomes in his efforts to make readers visit the pub. The speech that the system generates is modulated to reflect the current behavioural state of Lent. If he is "drunk", his speech will become slower, if he is agitated, his speech will accelerate and its pitch is raised.

Although there are aspects of this psychometric chatbot agent that Dare found useful, such as the authoring of a less deterministic deliberative agent, the greater value of creating this prototype has been in enabling Dare to identify its weaknesses and the weaknesses inherent in the conventions followed in the production of AI programs. Although Mateas's (1997) point that believability is not the same as realism is strong, Lent's anthropomorphised subjectivity is the central weakness of this program or indeed the disadvantage of its entire raison d'être. What would a program be like that attempted more profoundly to explore the asymmetries of machinic knowledge generation, the way that, for example, machines reason and process language, instead of covering up errors and asymmetries of understanding between computers and humans? What would it be like to cultivate those qualities as cultural traits and medium-specific distinct materialities of the agent medium and even more radically of psychometrics and proctoring software?

Dare's work with systems which attempt to generate subjective insight and which are therefore in some ways close to psychometric systems and allow us to ask what is personality and ethically and methodologically question the normative model of behaviour trust upon us and ask who has defined such traits as desirable and what function does empathy serve within such a monitored technological system. The following section considers these questions further in relation to personality testing and the tarot.

Personality testing versus the tarot

In this section, we present the findings of our investigation into the notion that Personal Construct Theory ignores inconvenient or messy variables that are not reconcilable with a narrow conception of rationality or of rational subjects. To do so, we approached *Feather Tarot*, a Berlin-based professional card reader, to ask if she could put the questions asked of Yamada-Rice during a personality test, undertaken during the application process for an academic role in a UK university, to the tarot. The intention was to understand the similarities and differences between the two sets of outputs and critique the so-called validity of such psychometric testing in HE. The areas asked to the tarot were the same as those in the NEO-PI-R Personality Inventory (Costa & McCrae, 2006) that Yamada-Rice completed first. These were:

1 Effectiveness at organising thoughts
2 Open-mindedness and originality
3 Confidence in problem-solving
4 Action Orientation
5 Conscientiousness
6 Openness to possibilities and alternatives
7 Social energy

8 Attitude to others
9 Quality of relationships
10 Level of emotionality
11 Pattern of emotions

Feather Tarot did not know Yamada-Rice had undergone the NEO-PI-R Personality Inventory (Costa & McCrae, 2006) and was also not privy to the results obtained before her reading. During the tarot reading, *Feather Tarot* placed a note with one of the 11 areas outlined above on a table in front of her. After consulting the tarot, she arranged the cards that answered the questions face up on a table in front of her. *Feather Tarot*'s readings were video-recorded from a bird's-eye view angle. Then, in order to compare them with the results of the NEO-PI-R Personality Inventory test which were disseminated as a written report with graphs, the video data were transcribed verbatim and still images of each hand of cards inserted into the transcript. Once this was done, both the report and the transcript were treated as individual datasets and both were analysed comparatively using thematic analysis (Braun & Clark, 2006) to draw out emerging themes. The remainder of this section reports on four themes that emerged from this analysis: (1) the whole self, (2) sole responsibility for your actions, (3) differences in what is valued and (4) the metrics of dissemination. These are discussed next.

The whole self

The first point to note is that the tarot reading began with an overview of Yamada-Rice's general personality traits (Figure 3.2). *Feather Tarot*'s reading of the cards presented Yamada-Rice as a being with two sides: on the one hand, the positive traits that can come when she is "feeling well and supported", and on the other, the negatives that arise when the opposite is true. *Feather Tarot* stressed that these traits are the fundamental principles on which Yamada-Rice's actions are framed.

By comparison, the psychometric analysis was concerned with Yamada-Rice in relation to other people it considers a comparable "reference group":

> Your responses have been compared with those of a reference group named: 'Total Sample (UK working population and job applicants). In this way we have been able to bench mark various

Figure 3.2 Tarot reading: personality traits.

characteristics you possess against this group. If we had used a different group for comparison, the analysis of your results might have turned out differently.

(Costa & McCrae, 2006, n.p)

As was stated in the literature review, making comparisons is problematic because the algorithms on which the test is based are not made up of the population at large but of subgroups, which are not explicit in the test itself, but "are in fact specific characteristic of corporate organisations" (Hollway, 1984, p. 56) and unclear to the examinee.

Feather Tarot stated that the underlying personality traits (Figure 3.2) are needed in order to understand the responses to the questions that will be asked of the cards about specific aspects of Yamada-Rice's approach to work. In other words, the personality traits offer insight into the reasons for the outcomes of the questions asked to the tarot about her attitude to her occupation. By comparison the NEO-PI-R personality test responses were not concerned with any external factors that might be involved in Yamada-Rice's way of responding to different aspects of her work. An example of this is in the response to the question of the level of emotionality Yamada-Rice has towards her work.

The psychometric test report presented the answer in the format of a graph shown in Figure 3.3.

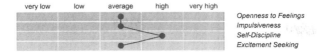

Figure 3.3 NEO-PI-R Personality Test: level of emotionality.

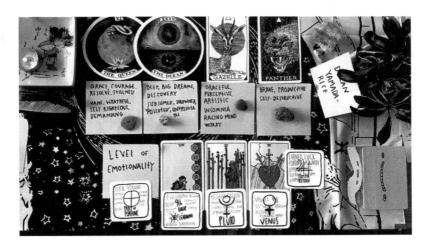

Figure 3.4 Tarot reading: level of emotionality.

And a written statement:

You are as attuned to your emotions as most people. Your feelings are likely to be a factor in the decisions you make, but you are not overly emotional. You are not an impulsive person nor are you overly controlled. You can tolerate frustration, and delay satisfaction of your needs, to the same extent as most people. Your level of need for environmental stimulation and excitement is within the average range for the reference group.

(NEO-PI-R personality test report for Yamada-Rice)

Whereas, analysis of the tarot card reading (Figure 3.4) was more complex and indicated the level of emotional impact her work could take on her:

Her emotions do not deter her from working no matter what but she is very affected by work. Work can really hurt her. She has heart breaking pain because of past work experiences. (Feather Tarot)

Fleming's (2021) book "Dark Academia" describes the extremity of the pressures faced by contemporary academics, even outlining the above-average statistics of self-harm and suicide in the sector. As a result, only considering the one-way effect of an employee on their work and institution should be seen as unethical. This is highlighted in more detail in the next section, which considers differences between the tarot and NEO-PI-R Personality Test in framing responsibilities for behavioural actions.

You are wholly responsible for your actions

The next striking difference between the two "tests" was that the tarot places some of the responsibility for how the human responds to work on factors outside of their control, whereas the psychometric test frames it as the entire responsibility of the academic:

> Human characteristics have the potential to be both assets and liabilities. The important thing is to recognise how you can capitalise on the benefits while minimising the disadvantages. The extent to which any particular characteristic is an advantage or a liability will depend on the context in which it is being applied. This report takes no account of contexts is it will be up to you to decide the extent to which the impact of your style in advantageous to the situation you are in (or aspire to be in).
>
> (Costa & McCrae, 2006)

This follows a trend in the neoliberal academy of placing all responsibility, even that of employee well-being, away from the institution and on to individual staff, while Fleming (2021) writes that universities desperate to be 'construed in a virtuous light [put on] "R U OK Day" and well-being programmes are celebrated by HR' (p. 36). Our experience is that these amount to little more than online mandatory wellness training videos that advocate for stretching and breathing well. Indeed, during Mental Health Awareness Week 2021, while struggling to be paid as Visiting Lecturers due to the poorly managed financial systems of our institutions, we received an en masse HR email stating that it could be good for our mental well-being to take our online work meetings in nature that week.

Differences in what is valued

Analysis of the tarot in comparison to the psychometric test also illustrated that the values and traits included were not the same as one

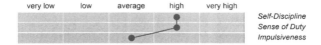

very low	low	average	high	very high	
			●		Self-Discipline
			●		Sense of Duty
		●			Impulsiveness

Figure 3.5 NEO-PI-R Personality Test: conscientiousness.

Figure 3.6 Tarot reading: conscientiousness.

another. The language used in the NEO-PI-R test was focused on pro-
ductivity. For example, Figure 3.5 shows how in relation to the trait
of conscientiousness the NEO-PI-R Personality Test was interested
in how the employee's personality would affect work output, however
the tarot reading focused on this in relation to colleagues and self-
fulfilment (Figure 3.6).

The psychometric test report stated:

> *You are unlikely to be deterred from carrying tasks through to com-
> pletion. Your self-discipline ensures that you will follow through de-
> spite any boredom or other distractions. You have the motivation to
> get the job done.*
>
> (NEO-PI-R personality test report for Yamada-Rice)

Indeed, the NEO-PI-R test report showed that within every category,
Yamada-Rice was compared to others:

When interacting with others, you are likely to be as friendly as most people.
(NEO-PI-R personality test report for Yamada-Rice)

Further, in all areas, this was quantified on a scale of "very low", "low", "average", "high" and "very high". This reflects differences in the epistemological and ontological framing between the two, with the NEO-PI-R framed as the rational and the tarot as irrational:

These cards may be consulted as subliminal objects, separate from rationality; they give access to magical environments…and entail a liberation from the rational corporeal form.
(Carrington, 2020, p. 11)

Such ideas link with the last theme about differences in the means of disseminating the outcomes of the psychometric test and tarot.

The metrics of dissemination

The NEO-PI-R disseminates its data through a series of charts and written statements, whereas:

In a tarot deck, the minor arcana may or may not be painted with images; however, the major arcana are almost always illustrated with fanciful, mythological, spiritual, and cultural imagery.
(Sosteric, 2014, p. 360)

The differences between illustration/paintings and graphs/writing are important when we consider Kress's (2010) notion that each mode of communication affords certain possibilities for the dissemination of information, and crucially that this is why certain histories and cultures favour some modes of communication above others. It is likely therefore that the differences in means of dissemination are not coincidental, but rather reference these historic and cultural values. Specifically, that graphs and writing represent the "rational" and that the illustrations in the tarot represent the irrational. This is what Campagna (2018) calls "technic" and "magic" terms he uses to illustrate opposite epistemological and ontological understandings of the world.

This section has attempted to critique the use of psychometric testing in HE by using an alternative form of personality testing in the form of tarot dating back to 1332 (Butler, 1975). Indeed, the history of the tarot shows how it came about:

> ...to ease the transition from pre-industrial structures of power and authority to industrial and bureaucratic structures. That tarot, associated as it was with the emergence of elite Freemasonry, helped provide new ideologies of power and ways of existing within new tightly structured, bureaucratic organizations.
>
> (Sosteric, 2014, p. 357)

We used the tarot not to ease the transition into the neoliberal structures of the university from what has gone before, but to highlight them. This was done to show the ridiculousness of using metrics to evaluate academics for roles in academia by showing how such tests, with their murky comparisons to reference groups that are not defined anywhere, should be held up to wider criticism. This is particularly important given Scott Galloway's prediction that the future of HE is in the collaborations that top universities will make with massive tech companies (Walsh, 2020), who routinely apply such data collection and analysis methods in their practices. Art universities, like the ones we belong to, are likely more susceptible than ever to such collaborations as they look to tech companies to help them fill the cut in funds made by governments.

The section has also shown how one of the most convenient omissions from the psychometric tests is the emotional side of being human. By contrast, we have shown how the tarot frames humans as emotional beings. In his book "Dark Academia", Fleming (2021) writes of the huge emotional and physical toll faced by academics as they navigate the neoliberal structures of contemporary HE. He is clear to state that this is because the current structures have been taken from business and marketing and are at odds with the traditional values of academics which are autonomy, research for the sake of knowing and slow thinking. In the next section, we show how drawing is a perfect medium for emotional expression and how it has acted as a mechanism for remaining sane within the neoliberal academy by allowing us to record our emotional responses to metrics and neoliberal structures.

Drawing: the antidote

In order to navigate the neoliberal structures of HE and the metrics we have been critiquing in this chapter, we have both at various points

Figure 3.7 Work allocation frameworks, Yamada-Rice.

during our working lives used drawing as an antidote. For Yamada-Rice, this takes the form of comics that record events and her emotional responses to them (Figures 3.7 and 3.8). As our discussion of psychometric testing in the last section suggests, the contemporary HE institute does not want the emotions of staff to enter the workplace. Yet the tarot frames humans clearly as emotional beings that can go in and out of balance depending on the pressures they face. Drawing has been described by many (e.g. McCloud, 1993) as affording the possibility for making emotions, which cannot be seen from the outside, visible.

Figure 3.7 records a conversation between an academic and their line manager in relation to metrics used to measure the allocation of their working time and the shift in duties of academics away from intellectual inquiry, which Fleming (2021) describes as being increasingly seen by their employers as an "indulgence" (p. 58):

Unlike values and language highlighted in the analysis of the NEO-PI-R Personality Inventory described previously, the drawing in Figure 3.7 feels more attune to Fleming's (2021) description of the relationship between staff and metrics:

After purchasing the advertised services from the brochure, the student- consumer is nominally 'empowered'/ They expect good grades and a well-paying job no matter what. This not only changes the relationship between teachers and student, but also academics and administrators. Given that customer satisfaction is essential, professional services staff invariably switch into de facto supervisors, sending a raft of demands, requests and requirements with firm deadlines.

(Fleming, 2021, p. 39)

Essentially, Figure 3.7 and Fleming are addressing the same point, but what is made visible is different. Kress (2010) talks about how the affordances of different modes enable the dissemination of some aspects of information but not others. Thus, it follows that drawing works to counteract the metrics used in the neoliberal university by making visible the parts of the system that they cannot show because "graphic representations can depict both concrete objects and symbolize abstract concepts at the same time" (Bowen & Evans, 2015, p. 53). With regards to comics specifically, Sousansis (2017) writes, "I knew well the sort of complex stories and ideas that could be addressed in comics" (p. 190).

In relation to his seminal graphic novel "Unflattening", Sousansis (2015) writes:

For Unflattening (as first conceived as a dissertation), I set myself some particular constraints from the start. I would name nothing. No field. No discipline. No philosophical movement. That didn't mean I wouldn't address them, but I would do so without using their language.

(Sousansis, 2015, p. 193)

In Figure 3.8, Yamada-Rice lifts the language of HE and places it in the wider context of world events to show how out of context they are with what is happening outside the academy:

Suwa and Tversky (1997) suggest that drawing provides a way of having a conversation with yourself. For Yamada-Rice, this opportunity to have a conversation with herself through drawing allows her to

Figure 3.8 Smile and the pandemic, Yamada-Rice.

make clearly visible that the underlying conditions in contemporary HE are not sustainable (e.g. Figure 3.9). This is important when we consider that between 2017 and 2019, UK universities spent £87 million on NDAs to prevent staff talking out about the harm done to them at work (Croxford, 2019). Work such as ours, shared here, stands in opposition to this, making the traumas suffered by academics visible.

As a final example, when recently asked to provide a linear account of her career, Dare produced Figure 3.10.

Dare's working life and practice has been far from the neatly discrete model found in psychometric and institutionalised constructs of subjectivity and work. Dare's work is positioned as diagrammatic, closer to an assemblage, a flow of data positioned between chaos and order. These are the conditions that Deleuze (1981) describes as being necessary for generating the new, in which the "diagram is indeed a chaos, a catastrophe, but it is also a germ of rhythm. It is a violent chaos in relation to the figurative given" (p. 72). Our experience of HE

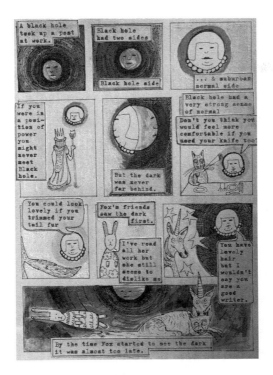

Figure 3.9 Black hole, Yamada-Rice.

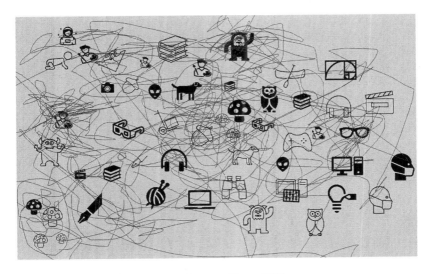

Figure 3.10 Academic career trajectory, Dare, 2021.

and its surveillant mechanisms have indeed been one of violent chaos, masked by an illusion of objective order.

Drawing like the chatbot created by Dare and the tarot reading undertaken by *Feather Tarot* offer mechanisms for knowledge that sits outside of mainstream metrics and AI systems increasingly being adopted by HE institutions. Yet, these three means of knowing the world also have a much deeper and longer history for meaning-making. In relation to drawing, Hoffman and Wittmann suggest that drawing is a common cultural technique and skill developed in childhood that it is so well known it "falls into the category of tacit knowing" (Hoffmann & Wittmann, 2013, p. 207). A tacit means of knowing, which Biederman et al. (2021) suggest, can be used as part of 'a "Great Refusal", the protest against that which is…that through art and this space of alterity enabled by an aesthetic dimension, a newly transformed world is possible' (p. 277). A view we feel offers hope to art schools in particular.

Conclusion

We began writing this chapter concerned with the neoliberal structures in universities, with a particular focus on the value attached to pseudo-scientific psychometrics and algorithms used to determine the value of its work place. Working together in an art school, where our practice as artists was important to our teaching and research outputs, we began to see how our preferred ways of knowing such as making, drawing and experimenting with materials, what Ingold (2013) calls knowing through our hands, were not valued in the structures that governed our outputs. However, these alternatives, coupled with others such as the development of critical chatbots and the tarot, are needed more than ever to critique HE practices because as others such as Fleming (2021) and Boyd (2020) are showing the current pandemic is highlighting the extreme extent of the weaknesses in the neoliberal structures we are working within. Like Boyd (2020) we believe that we are at a point in time where we need to consider 'what kind of world we want? …Nobody knows what is going to happen and that is all the more reason to fight for humane post-capitalist visions of the future' (n.p.).

References

Aarseth, E. J. (1997) *Cybertext: Perspectives on Ergodic Literature.* Baltimore: John Hopkins University Press.

Abercombie, R. (2015) *What No One Tells You about Psychometric Testing,* Recruiting Blogs, available at: https://recruitingblogs.com/profiles/blogs/what-no-one-tells-you-about-psychometric-testing [Accessed 02/08/21].

Alcoff, L. and Potter, E. (eds) (1993) *Feminist Epistemologies (Thinking Gender).* New York: Routledge.

Ansari, A. (2020) 'White Supremacy & Epistemic Colonialism in Design Discourse, Scholarship, & Practice: A Basic Primer', *Thread Reader,* available at: https://threadreaderapp.com/thread/1293262346761179137.html. [Accessed 02/08/21].

Barad, K. (2007) *Meeting the Universe Halfway, Quantum Physics and the Entanglement of Matter and Meaning.* Durham: Duke University Press.

Beiderman, K., Dare, E., Gordon, L., Ikoniadou, E., Lewis, M., Pochodzaj, J., Wee, C. and Yamada-Rice, D. (2020) 'Exercises in Exorcism- Ways of Healing (Through Art Eduction)' In: Benjamin, Ruha. *Race After Technology.* Medford, MA: Wiley. Kindle Edition.

Benjamin, R. (2019) *Race after Technology, Abolitionist Tools for the New Jim Code.* Cambridge: Polity Press.

Bowen, T. & Evans, M. M. (2015) 'What Does Knowledge Look Like? Drawing as a Means of Knowledge Representation and Knowledge Construction', Education for Information, Vol. 31 (1–2), pp. 53–72.

Boyd, R. (2020) 'Zoom and Gloom: Universities in the Ace of COVID-19'. *Los Angeles Review of Books,* available at: https://www.lareviewofbooks.org/article/zoom-and-gloom-universities-in-the-age-of-covid-19/ [Accessed 02/08/21].

Braidotti, R. (2002) *Metamorphoses: Towards a Materialist Theory of Becoming.* Cambridge: Polity Press.

Braun, V. and Clark, V. (2006) 'Using Thematic Analysis in Psychology', *Qualitative Research in Psychology,* Vol. 3 (2), pp. 77–101.

Browne, S. (2015) *Dark Matters, On the Surveillance of Blackness.* Durham and London: Duke University Press.

Butler, B. (1975) *Dictionary of the Tarot.* New York: Schocken Books.

Calvino, I. (1977) *The Castle of Crossed Destinies.* New York: Secker & Warburg Ltd.

Campagna, F. (2018) *Technic and Magic: The Reconstruction of Reality.* London: Bloomsbury.

Carrington, G. W. (2020) Leonora's Inner Compass, in Aberth, S. and Arcq, T. *The Tarot of Leonora Carrington.* New York: Fulgur Press.

Chomsky, N. (1999) *Profit Over People.* New York: Seven Stories Press. Kindle Edition.

ClassDojo (n.d) about, https://www.classdojo.com/

Costa, P. T. and McCrae, R. (2006) *NEO PI-R NEO Personality Inventory,* Revised UK edition, available at: https://www.hogrefe.com/uk/shop/neo-personality-inventory-revised-uk-edition.html [Accessed 01/08/21]

Croxford, R. (2019) UK Universities Face Gagging Order Criticism. *BBC,* available at: https://www.bbc.co.uk/news/education-47936662 [Accessed 29/7/21]

Deleuze, G. (1981) *Francis Bacon: The Logic of Sensation*. London: Continuum.
Demetriades, S., Kwong, J., Pearl, A. R., Thrupkaew. N., Maclay, C. and Pearlman, J. (2020) 'The Post-Pandemic Panopticon: Critical Questions for Facial Recognition Technology in Higher Education', Post-Pandemic University, available at: https://postpandemicuniversity.net/2020/10/11/the-post-pandemic-panopticon-critical-questions-for-facial-recognition-technology-in-higher-education/ [Accessed 02/08/21].
Dixon, T. (2012) "Emotion": The History of a Keyword in Crisis. 'Emotion Review. *Journal of the International Society for Research on Emotion*, Vol. 4 (4), pp. 338–344.
Eysenck, H. J. (1947) *Dimensions of Personality*. New Brunswick: Transaction Publishers.
Ferraro, D. (2014) Archives of a Divided Subject Psychology & Psychoanalysis in the 21st Century 'A Note on Psychometrics: A Critique of CBT as Ideology', available at: https://melbournelacanian.wordpress.com/2014/02/07/a-note-on-psychometrics-a-critique-of-cbt-as-ideology-part-4/ Accessed 05/01/2020. [Accessed 02/08/21].
Fleming, P. (2021) *Dark Academia: How Universities Die*. London: Pluto Press.
Haraway, D. (1991) *'The Cyborg Manifesto', from, Simians Cyborgs and Women: The Reinvention of Nature*. New York: Routledge.
Hayles, K. N. (1999) *How We Became Post Human*. Chicago and London: The University of Chicago Press.
Henriques, J., Hollway, W., Urwin, C., Venn, C. and Walkerdine, V. (1984) *Changing the Subject: Psychology, Social Regulation and Subjectivity*. London: Routledge, Reissued 1998.
Hoffmann, C. & Wittmann, B. (2013) 'Introduction: Knowledge in the Making: Drawing and Writing as Research Techniques', *Science in Context*, Vol. 26 (2), pp. 203–213.
Hollway, W. (1984) 'Fitting Work: Psychological Assessment in Organisations', in Henriques et al., *Changing the Subject*. London: Routledge, 1984, 1998, pp. 26–59. (reissued).
Illouz, E. (2007) *Cold Intimacies: The Making of Emotional Capitalism*. Cambridge: Polity. Kindle edition.
Ingold, T. (2013) *Making: Anthropology, Archaeology, Art and Architecture*. London: Routledge.
Johnson, K. (2020) 'Amazon Imposes One-year Moratorium on Police Use of Its Facial Recognition Technology', *Venturebeat.com*, available at: https://venturebeat.com/2020/06/10/amazon-imposes-one-year-moratorium-on-police-use-of-its-facial-recognition-technology/ [Accessed 02/08/2021].
Kress, G. (2010) *Multimodality: A Social Semiotic Approach to Contemporary Communication*. London and New York: Routledge.
Maes, P. (1994) 'Agents that reduce work and information overload', *Commun. ACM 37*, 7 (July 1994), 30–40.
Mateas, M. (1997) 'An Oz-Centric Review of Interactive Drama and Believable Agents', *cmu.edu*, available at: http://www.cs.cmu.edu/~michaelm/publications/CMU-CS-97-156.pdf

Mateas, M. (2001) 'Expressive AI: A Hybrid Art and Science Practice', *Leonardo*, Vol. 34 (2). pp. 147–153.

McCloud, S. (1993) *Understanding Comics: The Invisible Art*. Northampton, MA: Tundra.

Murad, A. (2020) 'The Computers Rejecting Your Job Application', *BBC News*, available at: https://www.bbc.co.uk/news/business-55932977

Murphy Paul, A. (2010) *The Cult of Personality Testing*. New York: Simon and Schuster.

proctortrack.com (2020) proctortrack.com, available at: https://www.proctortrack.com/blog/article/7-things-you-should-know-about-remote-proctoring/

Russell, S. and Norvig, P. (2002) *Artificial Intelligence: A Modern Approach* (2nd Edition). London: Prentice Hall Series in Artificial Intelligence.

Sosteric, M. (2014) 'A Sociology of Tarot', *The Canadian Journal of Sociology*, Vol. 39 (3), pp. 357.

Sousanis, N. (2017) 'Thinking in Comics: An Emerging Process.' In *Arts-based Research in Education*, edited by Melisa Cahnmann-Taylor and Richard Siegesmund, Chapter 16, pp. 190–200. New York, NY: Routledge.

Sousanis, N. (2015) *Unflattening*. Harvard: Harvard University Press.

Stengers, I. (2015) *Women Who Make a Fuss: The Unfaithful Daughters of Virginia Woolf*. Minnesota: Univocal Publishing.

Suwa, M. and Tversky, B. (1997) 'What Architects and Students Perceive in Their Sketches: A Protocol Analysis', *Design Studies*, Vol. 18, pp. 385–403.

Swauger, S. (2020) 'Software That Monitors Students during Tests Perpetuates Inequality and Violates Their Privacy', *MIT Technology Review*, August 7th 2020, available at: https://www.technologyreview.com/2020/08/07/1006132/software-algorithms-proctoring-online-tests-ai-ethics/

Walsh, J. (2020) The Coming Disruption: Scott Galloway Predicts a Handful of Elite Cyborg Universities Will Soon Monopolize Higher Education/ New York Magazine, available at: https://nymag.com/intelligencer/2020/05/scott-galloway-future-of-college.html

Wooldridge, M. (2009) *An Introduction to Multi-Agent Systems*. New York: John Wiley and Sons.

Index

Note: *Italic* page numbers refer to figures and page numbers followed by "n" denote endnotes.